On Afghanistan's Plains

Best wishes

Bay Alex

BARRY ALEXANDER

ISBN-10: 1532875282
ISBN-13: 978-1532875281

.

DEDICATION

For Lisa, who also served as she stood and waited

Dedicated to the memory of:

Captain David Charles Hicks MC
Private Tony Rawson
Corporal Barry Dempsey

CONTENTS

BARRY ALEXANDER

ACKNOWLEDGMENTS

Thanks to my wonderful wife Lisa and to Liberty, Tamsin and Benedict whose belief in my ability encouraged me to persevere with my writing. Special thanks to Tamsin for introducing me to Wattpad which enabled me to reach an audience for the first time. I also wish to thank Phil, Pete, Tom, Sam, Manie, Jamie, Steve, Matt and the countless other 'real' soldiers who looked after me 'over there' and are the true heroes of the story. Big thanks also due to 'JTAC Alex', our Joint Terminal Attack Controller, for his skill in ensuring that the bombs fell where they were supposed to. Sincere gratitude to John Jeffcock, whose poetry competition made me pick up my pen again. Thanks and best wishes go to Mary L Tabor, who has inadvertently become my mentor and a champion of my writing. Huge praise is due to Elaine Kennedy for her robust editorship and honest criticism which shaped the final version. Finally, thanks to James at GoOnWrite.com for the cover design.

This work is based on the author's experiences and recollections. Any inaccuracies stem from the his own fading memory. The author's opinions do not represent official views of the Ministry of Defence or the British Army.

1 BIRTH OF A SOLDIER

I think I was destined to join the army after being inspired by the images of Royal Marines and Parachute Regiment soldiers that flickered across the screen of our old black and white TV in the news coverage of the 1982 Falklands War. I was eleven years old then and the conflict seemed like an adventure straight out of one of those old-fashioned boys' comics that seem so dated nowadays. Between reports of the death of Lieutenant Colonel H Jones, killed while charging enemy trenches at Green, and the tale of Sergeant Iain McKay's death as he cleared the last of several machine-gun nests with grenades, my young mind was filled with romantic ideas of what soldiering was all about.

As I grew older, my understanding changed. Reading accounts of war, wounding and recovery by Robert Lawrence and Simon Weston made me realize that war was not all heroism, glamour and medals. This was also the era of Hollywood's depiction of the Vietnam War and the movies *Platoon*, *Full Metal Jacket* and *Hamburger Hill* delivered more graphic imagery and a more critical view of conflict than had the Allies vs. Germans offerings of the preceding decades. None of this deterred me from my calling to be a soldier.

Although I have only ever worn one uniform, I served in three Armies. The first was the Territorial Army (Reserves), which I joined aged seventeen and still at school. In the Territorials, I graduated from playing soldiers to training for war. It was the late 1980s, and the fear that Soviet hordes would descend on western Europe was still very real. Shortly before the collapse of the iron curtain, I spent a joyful couple of weeks on a NATO exercise in Germany which saw me dig trenches to defend the Sibbesse Gap against the Argyll and Sutherland

Highlanders and take part in a night-time crossing of the mighty river Weser in an assault boat that resembled a large tin bathtub. The river crossing was scary enough, but the punch-up with the Argylls as they cleared our main defensive positions was something else. There was blood and snot everywhere.

Although still convinced that I was going to be a soldier, I happened across nursing by accident and seemed destined for other things. However, I carried on in the Territorials to supplement the meagre pay of a student nurse while I completed my training.

The second army that I joined was the regular army, during the period following the cold war. In 1994 I walked through the gates of Whittington Barracks, Lichfield as a civilian and left ten weeks later as a trained soldier, passing out as Best Recruit of my intake.

Old Russia had imploded economically and politically and was no longer a threat while Saddam Hussein had lost 'the mother of all battles' four years earlier. The army that I had joined seemed to have no real enemies anymore. Although not entirely inactive, Irish Republican terrorists seemed to be in the mood for 'jaw-jaw' instead of 'war-war'. Apart from the ongoing peacekeeping operations in Cyprus and the Balkans, the army seemed to do little besides training exercises, daily PT, Friday morning eight-mile marches, Wednesday sports afternoons and drinking; lots of drinking. I spent seven years in that army and got to see and do most of the activities advertised in the glossy recruiting brochures of the era; these included dinghy sailing, scuba diving, parachuting, skiing and kayaking. Not only that, I got to travel to exotic places such as Norway, Canada, Belize, Cyprus and Aldershot. Okay, I lied; Belize is not that exotic.

During that time there were only a few occasions where I had a wake-up call to remind me what the army is actually about. I was shot at in Bosnia, and pretended to be a civilian nurse to conduct transfers of military patients to the secure ward of a civilian hospital in Belfast (on which occasions I was probably the only unarmed British soldier in west Belfast).

Each time the alarm rang, I pressed 'snooze' and carried on with my naïve uniformed existence. The last time this happened was when I found myself deployed to Sierra Leone in west Africa, to support a battalion of paratroopers who were evacuating British passport-holders from a country whose already fragile security situation was rapidly unravelling. Sierra Leone was an eye-opener, providing an unforgettable glimpse of the most savage aspects of human nature. These ranged from treating a teenaged girl shot several times while escaping a gang-rape perpetuated by an equally young group of rebels, to the suspected rebel subjected to interrogation by pistol at the hands of Nigerian 'peacekeepers'. I gather that the interrogation went something like this:

Nigerian soldier: "You're a rebel, aren't you?"

Captured man: "No, I'm just in this village to visit my girlfriend."

Nigerian soldier: (Draws pistol and shoots captured man in foot.) "You're a rebel, aren't you?"

Captured man: "No! I told you, I'm just visiting the village."

Nigerian soldier: (Shoots captured man in hand.) "I do wish you would stop lying. If you don't tell us the truth, the next bullet will go in your head!"

Captured man: "Oh, rebel, you say! Yes, silly me, how could I forget that? Yes, I think I am a rebel after all."

Nigerian soldier: "Hey, boss, come over here; this guy's a rebel!"

Nigerian officer: "Well, we'd better take him into the bush and shoot him then, hadn't we?"

At this juncture, the love-in was broken up by a British officer who intervened and insisted that the suspected rebel be taken to our medical section for treatment before being handed over to the Sierra Leone authorities. Although the captured man bore all the hallmarks of being a rebel, I have never forgotten the repugnance I felt at seeing such acts of barbarity committed by soldiers wearing the insignia of the United Nations. It is little wonder that, as we were then facing a numerically superior force of rebel fighters, our section had an agreement that in the event of imminent capture, we would kill as many of the enemy as possible and save the last bullet for ourselves.

After Sierra Leone, I pressed the 'snooze' button one last time, and woke up along with the rest of the world on Tuesday, September 11, 2001. On that morning, I was in California with two colleagues, four days into a period of Rest and Relaxation (R&R) from a seven-month detachment in Belize. Waking in our motel with hangovers resulting from a raucous night out in a whisky bar in Laguna Beach, we got up ready for some breakfast with the aim of being fit to drive north to San Francisco by noon.

One of the guys, Ed, switched on the TV. What appeared to be a 1970s disaster movie was playing, showing the World Trade Centre engulfed in flames. Our companion, Stretch, a straight-talking Devon lad stepped out of the shower and glanced at the TV. "Come on, lads, turn that fucking shit off and put the news on!" he said. I started to channel-hop. No matter which channel I selected, the same disaster movie was playing. "Fuck!" I gasped. "I think this *is* the news." All three of us stared incredulously at the TV screen, aware that something significant was happening but with no inkling of how it would come to shape our lives. Although I didn't yet realize it, I had just been discharged from the army of 'less interesting' times and transferred into an army on a campaign footing.

As the day wore on we went through with our plan to drive to San Francisco, arriving in the early evening. The city was quiet. Over the course of the day, the various fragments of news had tumbled around like a disordered kaleidoscope image until the view had cleared: someone (assumed to be Al Qaeda) had mounted an organised attack on the United States of America by hijacking three airliners and flying them into the iconic twin towers of New York's World Trade Centre and the Pentagon in Washington DC. A fourth jet had crashed in a field in Pennsylvania. Whilst the people around us were in a state of shock, Ed, Stretch and I sat in one of the few bars that were open, drank a few beers and began to contemplate what the attacks might mean for us as card-carrying members of the British Army.

There was no immediate change to a war footing. After the capture of Kabul by the Northern Alliance, aided by the US military, a succession of British units deployed to Kabul as part of the NATO-led International Security Assistance Force (ISAF). Over the years, there was an occasional roadside bomb, but for the most part Afghanistan largely became a forgotten deployment, overshadowed by the US-UK coalition invasion of Iraq and the subsequent insurgency and sectarian violence.

It was not until 2006 that Afghanistan registered in the public imagination, when the UK Secretary of State for Defence, Dr John Reid, announced the deployment of a British force into Helmand Province for a three-year period. Throughout the summer of 2006, troops from 16 Air Assault Brigade arrived with the intention of providing security for reconstruction only to find themselves dispersed in 'penny packets' across Helmand province and facing frequent attacks by large numbers of Taliban fighters. In the space of a few short weeks, the deployment in Helmand, known as Operation Herrick, became a shooting war. That summer, seventeen British soldiers were killed in action.

My first insight into the fighting came through reading an in-depth report by Christina Lamb of the *Sunday Telegraph*. This was the story of a routine patrol to the village of Zumbelay which became a fight for survival. From the comfort of the ante-room in the officers' mess at Catterick where I read the report, the fighting in Afghanistan seemed remote and distant.

Shortly after reading Lamb's article I was assigned to a new unit, a medical regiment (Field Unit) in Aldershot. On my arrival, I went through the usual arrival routine of having a *pro forma* document signed and stamped by various sub-units of the regiment to ensure that I was on everyone's radar. I was supposed to hand the completed form in to regimental headquarters within two weeks; instead, I did what I have done at every unit to which I have been assigned – I failed to hand the form in and then forgot about it. I found the form almost two years later, when I was clearing my desk to leave on another assignment. Everyone knows that the form that counts is the one that releases you from the regiment!

2 A WARNING OF WAR

The sergeant-major's voice echoes across the parade square, "Squadron, squadro-on, 'shun!" A millisecond later, one hundred left boots slam into the tarmac as the squadron snaps to the position of attention at the sergeant-major's command, each soldier growing in height as they stand with their necks in the back of their shirt collars, arms and legs braced rigid, shoulders back and chests pushed out.

The squadron commander, a major in the Royal Army Medical Corps, marches onto the square demonstrating his best 'drill face' and comes to a smart halt a couple of paces short of the sergeant-major. After an exchange of salutes, the sergeant-major informs our boss that the squadron is formed up and awaiting his disposal. The sergeant-major is asked to stand the squadron at ease and the order is given. One hundred left legs are swiftly raised, thighs parallel to the ground before the boots are once again driven into the ground with a satisfying crump. Our leader addresses us.

"Ladies and gentlemen," he begins, "it has been formally announced that the regiment will be supporting 12 Mechanised Brigade for a six-month tour of duty in Afghanistan, deploying in April next year. That gives us roughly six months of pre-deployment training. The pace of life will accelerate sharply. I am pleased to inform you that this squadron has been selected to perform a close support role for the tour. Many of you will be working in the most austere locations in direct support of the troops on the ground. There will be much more information forthcoming, but between now and deployment the commanding officer's direction is that we will work on our infantry skills, our fitness and our medical skills."

The brief address is over and, following another flurry of

salutes, the squadron commander takes his leave of us, handing back to the sergeant-major. The sergeant-major reads out a few 'parish notices' before bringing the squadron to attention and ordering the officers to fall out.

My fellow officers and I have been grouped in a single rank at the rear of the assembled squadron, which has formed up in three ranks. At the sergeant-major's command, we execute a sharp right turn before marching off three paces and moving swiftly away from the soldiers who remain on parade. Returning to our offices, we continue the day's work; in my case, the preparation of a team to deploy on a large exercise on Salisbury Plain in a week's time. Recently arrived in the unit, I have not yet been on exercise with the squadron and my initial impression is less than favourable.

Aside from a low-key peace support tour of Bosnia, the regiment has not deployed on operations since the invasion of Iraq in 2003, and many of the soldiers are inexperienced. Just after my arrival, there was a bit of a stir when the squadron was warned of an emergency deployment to Lebanon. In the event nobody went anywhere, but it was useful to see how poorly prepared some individuals were to depart at short notice into a hostile environment.

At this stage, I have been in the army as a nurse for twelve years; spending ten years in the ranks, progressing from private to sergeant, before becoming a commissioned officer two years ago. As a captain in my second appointment, I am now the training officer for A Squadron. At thirty-five years of age, I realize that for the first time I am just old enough to be a parent to the youngest of the soldiers. I now bear a responsibility to these young men and women and their families to ensure that they are as well prepared as possible for what they may face in the next twelve months.

The run-up to Christmas is taken up with a series of exercises and training packages. We find ourselves engaged in training on Salisbury Plain, Aldershot, Norfolk and Folkestone. One of the most memorable occasions is the final serial of a regimental exercise, which sees the officers' mess combine with the warrant officers' and sergeants' mess for a formal regimental dinner which is held under canvas in the field, complete with silver on the tables. After two weeks in the field we are tired and the alcohol, particularly the after-dinner port, is potent. I retire to my sleeping bag in the early hours of the morning and feel decidedly rough the next day. I am not the only person to be in a bad way, we later discover that at one point in the evening a bout of fisticuffs was broken up between two officers who should have known better.

On a succession of chilly autumn mornings, we find ourselves subjected to an increasingly demanding regime of physical training. We are repeatedly put through our paces over the large training area near our barracks. Most Friday mornings we have the joy of speed-marching and running while carrying full equipment over terrain that varies between flat but unyielding tarmac roads, rough tracks, some very steep inclines and tracts of ankle-deep porridge-like mud that is slippery enough to deny us traction, but with insufficient viscosity for us to get stuck. The training is challenging and there are always a few stragglers who drop their pace and need encouragement to keep going. The principal aims are to build our stamina to endure long patrols carrying full equipment and ensure that we are fit to withstand the demands that the Afghan climate will place upon our bodies. One day, we think we are going to have an easy ride when we are put on trucks to take us to the swimming pool to complete the army swimming test, which involves treading water for two minutes and a one hundred metre swim followed by an unaided exit from the pool without the use of the steps. Once we have completed the swimming test, instead of getting changed, we are directed to don combat uniform and get back in the pool with some dummy rifles for company. These mock-ups are mostly made of rubber but look and weigh the same as the real thing. The next hour is not so much swimming as not-drowning with rifles. I try several methods until I find that the best technique is to swim on my back with the rifle in one hand, it is a tough session, but I am quietly pleased when I make it all the way through without drowning or quitting. By the time we get out of the pool, quite a few people have dropped out and are sitting on poolside.

The commanding officer, a former gunner who is parachute- and commando-qualified, intends to drive the regiment to a peak of fitness in time for the deployment. The standard army test for a loaded march is eight miles covered in two hours. We take this as the starting point and push the envelope in terms of distance covered, time elapsed and weight carried. By Christmas we are routinely completing ten-mile marches and immediately launching into a mile-and-a-half best effort run, still wearing our loaded march kit and carrying rifles.

January sees us continuing our training with a live firing package in Otterburn, Northumberland, a beautiful but forbidding area of high moorland near the Scots Borders. The weather is predictably cold. Along with two corporals, Geordie and Richie, I am tasked with providing some team medic lectures and training to various units of the brigade. This training ensures that the soldiers are comfortable with the use of the combat application tourniquet and the new-fangled haemostatic agents, which help to prevent a wounded man from bleeding out (bleeding to death) and help to keep him alive for long enough to reach hospital care.

In between teaching, we are bussed out to take part in some live firing exercises, conducting small unit tactics against pop-up targets. It is hard work, but great fun. The exercise culminates in a loaded march out to a firepower demonstration intended to showcase the firepower that will be available to us in theatre.

Towards the end of our build-up phase, we take part in the mission rehearsal exercise, which is held on Salisbury Plain in bitterly cold weather. For much of this exercise I am based at Netheravon Camp with a small team of medics, where we are tasked with playing the role of the Medical Emergency Response Team (MERT). The role of the MERT is to deploy from Camp Bastion by helicopter to retrieve casualties, provide advanced trauma care and transport them to the field hospital. In Afghanistan, the MERT is crewed by a senior emergency medicine or intensive care doctor, an emergency department nurse, a paramedic and an operating department practitioner.

The casualty play is limited and sometimes farcical. On one occasion my team is poised to receive casualties from a helicopter, only to be presented with a sheet of A4 paper on which '2 x civilian amputees' has been scrawled in black felt pen. To say that I am deeply unimpressed would be an understatement. Our presence is of some use, however, when we have to deal with some genuine casualties: a soldier with suspected spinal injuries from a vehicle rollover and an Afro-Caribbean soldier with superficial frostbite sustained during a circuitous journey around the south of England, intended to recreate a logistic resupply convoy in Helmand.

When the exercise comes to an end, we return home for a couple of weeks leave and well-earned rest. The next trip away will be for six months and there will be no rest for a long time.

Throughout the run-up to deployment, I am plagued by an irrational fear that it will all be over by the time we get to Afghanistan. I don't know why I have these thoughts; the previous summer has seen an escalation of fighting in Helmand province that has continued through the winter. In the weeks before we deploy, a number of British troops are killed as a result of indirect fire attacks on static bases. The most common weapon system used for this type of attack is the 107-mm Chinese rocket. Despite my concerns, the evidence stacks up against me – Afghanistan has been in a near-constant state of conflict since the Soviet Russian invasion in 1979. This is not going to be over any time soon. You would think that I would be relieved if it was to all be over, but the naïve young kid inside me wants to see a bit more action before I am too old.

Reality sets in soon enough. As deployment looms, the tension at home rises to a point at which the sooner I leave, the better it will be for all of us. I'm not easy to live with and I constantly battle with the fear that I'll come home severely wounded or in a casket draped with a Union Jack. What I want is to go there, get the job done and return home. I spend long periods of time gazing at my baby boy as he sleeps in his cot; vowing that, barring cowardice and dereliction of duty, I will stop at nothing to ensure that I return home alive. I will kill any enemy who threatens to stand between me and a safe homecoming; having a wife and family will make me fight harder.

Despite it being late March, the week prior to our departure sees the south of England covered in a dusting of snow. The officers' mess stages a final pre-deployment social event which consists of a visit to the Hunterian museum of the Royal College of Surgeons in Lincoln's Inn Fields, cocktails in the American bar at the Savoy Hotel followed by a dinner at Nobu in Mayfair, where we have the privilege of enjoying a private dining room.

This restaurant is famous for two reasons: the first is its high-end Japanese cuisine, the second is the fact that its rest-room was the setting for the impromptu act of intimacy which resulted in Boris Becker's equally high-end paternity suit. The food is exotic and delicious, but does nothing to soak up the alcohol already consumed or to counteract the strong saki wine and Japanese beer that we are drinking. The adjutant is allergic to fish and is severely pissed off at the imbalance between the cost of the meal and the range of dishes that he can eat. Another officer is so drunk that he resembles an empty wetsuit carelessly discarded half on and half off the table. We deploy days later.

One of the last things I need to do before leaving is to get a haircut. Our neighbour's wife offers to give me a trim. She usually does her husband's haircuts, has a set of clippers and claims that she used to be a hairdresser.

It starts off well, but while she cuts my hair, the lady is chatting to my wife and is apparently incapable of multi-tasking. The guard falls off the clippers momentarily and I end up with 'number two' on the sides and back, plus a bonus two-inch by one-inch rectangle of 'number zero' on the back of my head. Outwardly I am polite about the mistake and appear to take it in good humour; inwardly, however, I am incandescent with rage. Were Quentin Tarantino to direct the movie of my life, I would be describing myself to the lady as a 'mushroom cloud-laying motherfucker.' I should opt for the sensible course of action and get shorn to the wood all over, but of course I don't. Instead, I choose to walk around looking like a complete twat until the hair grows back.

On the day that we leave, I have to report to barracks in the small hours of the morning. As my wife drives me there, I feel drunk with fatigue. The sadness of our parting hangs so heavily that barely a word passes between us. We pull up in the car park and hold each other tightly, neither of us wanting to let go. Eventually we have to say goodbye; I grab my kit and equipment from the boot of the car and we walk together to the guardroom to have my name checked off the list. One final long hug and it is time to part. Words don't come easily and tears prick at my eyes as the enormity of this undertaking finally hits home. I am not new to soldiering; I have been shot at and faced up to threats ranging from terrorism to minefields, but Afghanistan promises to take these experiences and raise them by several notches. One last lingering kiss and I board the minibus.

We are driven from Aldershot to the air mounting centre in South Cerney and take the opportunity to sleep as best we can. On arrival, we have a cup of shit 'cofftea' (warm liquid that resembles a combination of coffee and tea) and play the age-old soldiers' game of 'hurry up and wait'. Two things occur to keep the campers happy.

The first is the appalling delivery of the brief by the movements control staff, Territorial Army (Reservist) soldiers who have been mobilised for the deployment. The female soldier delivering the brief can barely string a sentence together and is clearly terrified by the prospect of speaking in front of a large number of people. I do feel sorry for her, but cannot keep a straight face as the brief becomes a series of malapropisms, bringing new words to the English language.

The second thing that brightens the dreary night is that, as we sit receiving the brief, someone notices my dodgy haircut. When my colleagues hear my tale of woe, they genuinely sympathise with me and tell me not to worry about it and that it could happen to anyone. Really? No, of course they don't. They take the piss out of me mercilessly, just as I would do to any one of them. All is fair in love and war and a shit haircut is a shit haircut. I get what I deserve for not having shaved it all off.

After a long night of impenetrable briefings, weighing of kit, piss-taking and trying to sleep on hard plastic chairs, we go to the cookhouse for a shit breakfast before boarding a double-decker bus that will take us to RAF Brize Norton. In the drab half-light of a grey morning, the usually picturesque Oxfordshire landscape of Cotswold stone villages and farmland lacks appeal. As we pass through Lechlade on Thames, I think of my brother who lives in a nearby village and envy the fact that he is a 'gentleman still abed' and will never know the bittersweet taste of cherished kisses before a journey to distant battlefields. Although I was drawn to an army career by the prospect of a life untainted by the dull drudgery of the routine, at this precise moment a nine-to-five job of brain-numbing tedium seems very attractive.

We arrive at Brize Norton and endure a protracted period of time during which the RAF seems to do its best to fuck us about. Processed into the departure lounge, we sit for ages until we are told that there is a fault with the aircraft. This unexpected hiatus sees us driven to Gateway House, an all-ranks transit accommodation facility resembling a crap 1980s hotel, where we are given more refreshments. This is clearly an attempt to look after us, but coming so soon after the breakfast at South Cerney, I am in danger of feeling like a funnel-fed duck being fattened for *foie gras*.

Eventually, we return to the terminal and board the

aircraft. The flight carries troops from all units deploying into theatre, the idea being to have a mix of units on each flight so that if there is a crash, the military won't lose entire units or key individuals in one go. I sit down and cringe when I hear the voice of a young soldier calling out from several rows behind me.

"Fucking hell!" says the voice. "Look at the state of that bloke's haircut!"

I ignore the comment, insert my headphones and fill my ears with Beethoven and my mind with Afghanistan. It's going to be a long flight.

3 ARRIVAL

We land at Kandahar airfield in the early hours of the morning. After being processed through the prefabricated building that passes for an arrivals lounge, we are bussed to the transit accommodation, a huge temporary structure filled with bunk beds. Everyone else who has arrived on the same flight is also trying to get a bed space and a chance to sleep. Despite having slept for a good deal of the journey, I am still tired and it is a joy to get out my sleeping bag and stretch out on the plastic-covered bare mattress. I'm sound asleep within minutes.

Several hours later, I'm awoken by the scream of fast jets taking off; it is dawn. Rising, I pack away my kit and go in search of somewhere to get a shower and shave; I'm directed to a nearby complex of Portakabin-type accommodation which has civilised ablution facilities. Ten minutes later, I emerge, clean and refreshed, complete with fresh socks and underpants. A few others from my unit are also up and about, including the regimental sergeant-major (RSM) and the adjutant. We elect to go for a wander, explore Kandahar airfield and find some breakfast.

Breakfast is served in the DFAC, which is US-speak for cookhouse. We have to turn in our day-sacks at the entrance to the facility and soon discover the reason why. Inside there are a number of large refrigerators well stocked with Gatorade, Coca-Cola, lemonade and all sorts of other sodas. In keeping with their reputation for liberating anything that isn't nailed down, British troops have a habit of filling their day-sacks with enough drinks to last a week. As well as soft drinks, the variety, quantity and quality of food on offer is amazing compared to British cookhouses.

After a good meal, we resume our tour of Kandahar. We

find our way to the Boardwalk, a raised wooden walkway which, if viewed from above, would look like a large hollow square. The Boardwalk is home to a number of retail outlets in Portakabin or static trailer buildings. There is a vendor of Persian carpets, a number of shops selling souvenir T-shirts and military gear as well as some food outlets - Pizza Hut, KFC and a Tim Horton's coffee shop. Elsewhere on the base, there's a US PX and a Canadian Can-Ex, a Green Bean café and a Costa coffee outlet. This leads us to the conclusion that anyone spending their entire tour in Kandahar would have to live like a monk and work out constantly in the gym to avoid coming home flat broke and overweight.

We spend the rest of the morning killing time, enjoying the delights of Kandahar, until it's time for us to board a C-130 transport plane for the twenty-minute flight to Camp Bastion. We sit crammed into the nylon web seats wearing our helmets and body armour. This is the first time on the tour that I play the 'what if?' game, in which I confront myself with various scenarios, the actions I could take under such circumstances and the potential outcomes, good or bad. The most obvious concern is the plane being shot down. Should that happen, I seriously doubt that my body armour and helmet will be of much use; I wonder if I shouldn't follow Hollywood's example and sit on my helmet to save my balls from being blown off. In the end, I decide that my brain is more important than my balls and keep my helmet on my head. The next nightmare scenario would be to survive a crash and be thrust into a survival situation with the added complication of being pursued by a couple of hundred angry Taliban. Although the Pashtun honour code demands that strangers are given hospitality, I doubt that this will be extended to a British soldier. Somewhere beneath our flight path is the site of the Battle of Maiwand, in which our forebears suffered a humiliating defeat during the Second Afghan War. Here, as in many other parts of the world, Brits are not welcome and should one fall into hostile hands, a quick death would be a mercy that one would not anticipate.

Fortunately, the flight passes without event and before long the aircraft is in a steep descent to make the short landing onto the airstrip at Camp Bastion. We are taken by bus to our new base and told that our baggage will follow. Arriving at Brydon Lines, we are given a very short tour and shown to our tents in the temporary desert accommodation (TDA).

Our unit is in the process of taking over from our predecessors from the 3 Commando Brigade medical squadron and for the next week, the population of the TDA will be very transient with old sweats returning from the field at the end of their tour and new kids on the block arriving from the UK. I share a tent with seven other officers and, once we have received our kit, I start to sort out my life.

For those of us who are going out into the field, one of the main challenges is to choose what we will be take and which items will be left locked in the storage container at Camp Bastion. We are limited to what we can carry and a balance has to be struck between mission essentials and creature comforts. The personnel for whom Camp Bastion will be home for six months merely have to wait for a permanent bed space.

Over the next two days, we attend a reception, staging and onward integration (RSOI) training course, which consists of a fun-packed day of death by PowerPoint and a short range package. Most of the content is a reinforcement of what we have learned in our pre-deployment training, and the jetlag and tiredness from the protracted journey take their toll. Before long, most heads in the room loll at least once as their owners doze off when a long blink lasts longer than intended. The final briefing of the day commands our attention - the improvised explosive device and landmines threat brief from the Royal Engineers.

I sleep soundly that night, but it appears that my colleagues do not: I wake to find my camp cot surrounded by a number of boots that have been hurled in my direction during the night. Whilst I am aware that I snore, I didn't think I was that bad! For the rest of the tour, I make sure that I don't sleep on my back. I think back to an occasion seven years beforehand, when I was with a group of about one hundred and fifty soldiers sleeping in a factory building near Tromso in the north of Norway. After a couple of minutes of low mumbling and murmuring in his sleep, one of our medics sat bolt upright in his sleeping bag, fast asleep but with his eyes open, and proceeded to scream his head off. It was a surreal experience and people were sympathetic the first night. When the same lad started with the murmuring again the following night, a voice from across the room told him in no uncertain terms to shut up and lie down. So abrupt an instruction, accompanied by a clear threat of violence ensured that the medic did not scream on that night or any other. I wonder if I will get a dose of similar medicine to cure me of my snoring?

After an early breakfast we draw out our weapons from the armoury, a shipping container containing some rifle racks, and make our way to the one-hundred-metre range at the back of camp. We test-fire our rifles and re-zero them, to ensure that our optical sights are in alignment with our fall of shot. It wouldn't do to accidentally hit a non-combatant!

The shoot is over by lunchtime and, as we walk back into Camp Bastion in the midday heat, I start to get an indication of the temperatures that will face us as we move into summer. We drink plenty of water and have a good lunch before cleaning our rifles. For the guys deploying to the outposts, there is a good chance that the next time we fire our rifles will be in self-defence.

The afternoon is spent receiving some medical refresher training along the lines of the Battlefield Advanced Trauma Life Support course. The main areas for revision include the use of some of the most modern and innovative items of equipment and techniques. A Royal Air Force Paramedic from the MERT takes us through a refresher on intra-osseous access (inserting a hefty needle into the bone marrow of the sternum or tibia to provide fluid replacement therapy and pain relief). This technique is regarded as the best method of accessing the circulatory system if you cannot find a vein. The tools to do the job are quite brutal; there is an electric hand drill to place the needle into the tibia and a spring-loaded 'gun' to push the needle into the sternum.

In another session we are taken through the use of the novel haemostatic agents by a very eminent military trauma doctor, who ranks in the top tier of his profession internationally. The novel haemostatics agents are designed to stop bleeding at limb junctions in a matter of minutes. Historically, these have been the types of wound that cause soldiers to bleed to death on the battlefield for want of a trauma surgeon. If you recall the scene from the movie *Black Hawk Down* in which a young soldier dies as a result of bleeding out from a bullet wound to the groin you will get the picture.

There are two types of haemostatic agent demonstrated to us: one is for use on bleeding from the veins, another for the arteries. When a vein is severed, dark red blood pours from the wound in a steady gush. This type of bleed is stopped using a powder derived from volcanic ash, which, when poured onto the bleeding point, forms a plaque and arrests the haemorrhage. Bleeding from arteries is bright red due to the high oxygen content and pumps out of the severed vessel with spurts that coincide with each beat of the victim's heart. We are cautioned to avoid using this substance on spurting arterial bleeds because, when the powder comes into contact with blood, it causes an exothermic reaction (the blood gets hot before coagulating). As a result, there is a risk that the patient's surrounding skin may be scalded by splashes of hot blood, quite literally adding insult to injury. Arterial wounds are best treated by the second agent, which is derived from crustaceans and impregnated into gauze pads. The gauze pads are applied directly to the bleeding vessel and can stop the bleeding within seconds, although we are trained to apply direct pressure over the pad for two minutes. Months later I read an article by a military orthopaedic surgeon, in which he criticises the haemostatic agents for making the surgeon's job more difficult. I hope that someone in a position of authority gently reminds him that without the haemostatic agents, he might not have a live patient on which to operate.

After our medical training is complete, we have another briefing. Before arriving in Afghanistan, the squadron commander, his commissioned officers and senior non-commissioned officers held many conferences to decide which troops would deploy to which outstation locations. The decision-making process was founded upon assessment of three factors: clinical competence, military skills and physical fitness. By the time of our arrival, the squadron's medics have been sorted into three cohorts – those who can be sent to austere and demanding outposts, those who may go to the larger (and presumably more benign) bases and those who must remain in Camp Bastion for remedial medical, physical or military training.

Two events occur which make it necessary to recalculate. The first is the commencement of Operation Silver, a large operation intended to clear the Taliban out of Sangin district centre. The Taliban have held sway in Sangin for too long, and it has been decided that step one of the fight back for this year will be to give them a bloody nose and push them out. Some of our most capable guys are sent to Sangin in support of the operation; they leave that night.

The second change is to the order in which units are sent out on the ground. There is a rush to get rifle companies to particular locations in a different sequence to that envisaged. Some of the medics who've been earmarked for these locations have not yet arrived in theatre, which means that Plan A is flexed to meet the requirement. I thought I would be deploying on the ground within twenty-four hours of my arrival; instead I have to hang around Camp Bastion for a few days waiting to get out to the sharp end.

Along with Pete, a fellow nursing officer, I wave off the Sangin team as they climb aboard the transport that will take them to the helipad. Long before he became a nurse, Pete was a Parachute Regiment soldier. As a youngster, he fought in the Falklands when I was a wee lad in short trousers. Pete is a grumpy old bugger, but likeable nonetheless. We have not yet had our deployments confirmed and are a little bit envious of the men going out before us. As the Land Rover disappears into the distance, we stop waving, look at each other and simultaneously say 'Lucky bastards', before pissing ourselves laughing.

4 C COMPANY

Over the next few days, there is nothing to do but kill time in Camp Bastion. I pack, unpack and repack my field kit until I am satisfied that I have everything that I'm going to need and am content with where it all is. We hand in our combat body armour and Mark 6 helmets, exchanging them for the new-fangled Mark 6 Alpha (don't you just love the imaginative military naming conventions?) and Osprey body armour.

Compared with their predecessors, both items of kit represent a significant improvement in ballistic protection. The old combat body armour is fitted with two ballistic plates, about six inches square and a half-inch thick. In contrast, the Osprey has large plates that cover most of the upper torso at the front and back. If you are vehicle-bound, paranoid or can afford the additional weight and reduced mobility, you can fit the small combat body armour plates into the sides of the Osprey to give yourself some flank protection. There are also a neck protector and arm guards, if you want the whole Robocop look.

I leave behind the neck protector and arm guards, opting to carry the big plates only. Even without the additional protection, the Osprey armour is a substantial burden which, added to the weight of my patrol kit, makes for a very heavy load. The question on everyone's mind is whether we're better off without all the protective kit and therefore able to move faster. As I have yet to meet anyone who can run faster than 7.62-mm bullets, I am firmly in the camp of favouring protection over mobility … for now.

Although it is still springtime, the days are considerably hotter than at home; so, to aid my acclimatisation, I take to running in the early afternoons. There are a number of running routes around the base: my preferred option is the camp perimeter, which is about four miles. Before I have many runs under my belt, I am given the nod that there is some news about my deployment. As expected I am heading for Kajaki, in the far north of Helmand province, with Geordie, a gregarious and highly competent medic. Geordie and I have worked together over the course of the pre-deployment training; despite our difference in rank, we have a bond of mutual respect that borders on friendship.

We are briefed that we are deploying in support of C (Essex) Company of the 1st Battalion, the Royal Anglian regiment. Known by the nickname 'Vikings', this battalion recruits from East Anglia and has antecedents dating back to the earliest origins of the formation of a standing army in the 17th century. The Vikings are so called because their recruiting area is that part of England which in Anglo-Saxon times was apportioned to Viking settlers, known as the Danelaw.

Together, Geordie and I head over to the large transit block in which C Company is accommodated. We enter the block to be greeted by the sight of a large number of troops sorting their lives out. I grab a young soldier and ask to be directed to his company commander. The soldier points out a wiry, tough-looking man with dark hair. Geordie and I introduce ourselves and we have a short chat. It soon transpires that we have been directed to the wrong company commander; both B and C companies are in this building. Mick, the officer commanding B Company, directs us towards a handsome young man on the other side of the room.

We repeat our introductions, this time to the appropriate officer. The first thing that strikes me about this young man is his ready smile and friendly demeanour. He shakes my hand and introduces himself as Dave Hicks. We are soon joined by an older man; lean, with a weather-beaten and suntanned face, this is Pete, C Company's company sergeant-major (CSM). We talk over a few issues. I am most concerned with gaining an insight into the most likely (non-combat) medical issues I might encounter and gauging how welcoming the company hierarchy will be towards outsiders. I have worked with the infantry on several occasions over the years and have learned the hard way that the tribal nature of the British regimental system means that outsiders are not always welcome.

I needn't have worried; it is apparent that Dave and the CSM are both very pleased to have additional medical support embedded into the company. It is equally reassuring to sense the air of calm professionalism permeating this group of soldiers as they prepare for operations. The CSM admits that there are a lot of young lads in the company, but he is convinced they will do well. We are due to leave by helicopter the following morning, so Geordie and I make arrangements to meet the company at the helipad. Both men exude an air of laid-back confidence and I leave their accommodation with the impression that C Company is well-trained and well-led.

The following morning, Geordie and I are out of bed early and go to breakfast. We have no idea what the food is going to be like at Kajaki, so we make the most of what could be our last decent meal. Shortly after breakfast we sign out our rifles, ammunition and controlled medications before being driven to the helipad. Geordie admits that he suffers from a fear of flying and is 'fucking terrified' at the prospect of flying to Kajaki. I retort that it is a long way to walk, which makes us both laugh.

We meet up with the men of C Company at the helipad and, after the obligatory half-hour wait in the sun, board a waiting Chinook helicopter and take off into the white heat of the late morning. The flight only takes forty minutes, but it feels as though we are flying to the edge of the universe. From now until the end of our time in Kajaki, Britain will consist of ourselves and the men on either side of us. Beyond the forward line of our own troops will be hostile territory: the domain of terrorists, warlords, jihadists and a whole load of ordinary people stuck in the middle, trying to live their lives without pissing off anyone who carries a weapon.

5 KAJAKI

After about thirty minutes in flight, the Chinook banks to the left and reduces altitude. Most of us on board are craning our necks to get a glimpse of the ground. To the left of the aircraft lies a long spur of high rocky outcrops; on the opposite side, a patchwork of arable fields stretches to the horizon. As the aircraft continues to bank, we notice a clear sign that we are nearing our drop-off point: the still waters of the Kajaki Lake which shimmer in the morning sunshine. As we fly over its southern edge, the change in light reflection turns the lake from a brilliant quartz colour to a beautiful emerald. With no camera to take a photo, I commit to memory this image of serene beauty.

The loadmaster holds up two fingers to give us a two-minute warning. Throughout the helicopter men are fighting to stand up, lift their rucksacks onto their backs and grab their personal weapons. It is vital that we disembark as rapidly as possible to minimise the risk of the helicopter being attacked by enemy mortar or rocket fire. Within minutes of touching down we have exited the aircraft, two lines of waiting troops have climbed on board to take our place and the aircraft has gone wheels up to make the return flight to Camp Bastion.

As the Chinook heads into the distance, we gather our kit and load it onto a trailer attached to a Pinzgauer utility vehicle. Squeezing into the back of the Pinzgauer, we make the short trip to Combat Outpost Zeebrugge, so named by the Royal Marines from whom we are taking over, after one of their many memorable battle honours.

Arriving at COP Zeebrugge, there appears to be some confusion. The outgoing Royal Marines company had a larger medical team, consisting of two company medics and two medics who were allocated to the operational mentoring and liaison team (OMLT – pronounced 'omelette'). The incoming medical team consists of Geordie and myself, each with the expectation of providing medical support to the rifle company, whilst the OMLT colour sergeant from the Grenadier Guards, believes that we should be supporting his team.

The matter is referred to Phil, the company commander, sometimes known as 'Angry Phil'. A tallish man with a shaved head, Phil's decision confirms my thoughts. It is agreed that my team will provide support to the OMLT (and the Afghan national army platoon for which they are responsible) as well as to C Company. We will base ourselves at the company's medical facility and visit the OMLT/ANA compound to see patients on request. Any urgent or trauma cases will be brought to our facility.

The fact that I am a nursing officer also causes some confusion. The infantry are used to having medical officers (doctors) and medics; during the early stages of the tour, I struggle to get the troops to understand that I am not a doctor. Numerous conversations with soldiers in which I explain that I am a nurse end with them replying "Okay, Doc." One day Phil asks me to explain the differences in capability between a doctor, a nurse and a medic. There are differences not just in knowledge and skills, but also in mind-set; some of these can be quite subtle and nuanced, and I struggle to articulate them sufficiently well to give Phil the clear-cut answer he is looking for.

After humping our kit into the medical facility, Geordie and I start to make ourselves at home. The medical room is large enough to have two stretchers set up side by side and has fixed shelving on three walls, on which various packages of medical equipment and pharmaceuticals are laid. The walls are rendered smooth with plaster and the bare concrete floor is laden with dust and sand.

At one end of the room, next to the door, sits a tatty two-seat sofa upholstered in blue leather, along with some camp stools and fold-up chairs. This area serves as both our waiting room and communal space. Off the main room is a narrow corridor running left to right; to the right is my room, adjacent to Geordie's. At the other is a kitchen and another bedroom, earmarked for the two military policemen who are expected to arrive in the next few days.

On the evening of our arrival, Phil gathers the officers and senior non-commissioned officers for a briefing. Before the company starts patrolling, there will be a couple of days training which will consist of a round robin of specialist weapons familiarisation, demolitions and medical training, for which Geordie and I will be responsible. I want to ensure that the men are all confident in the application of the combat application tourniquet (CAT), can apply an emergency care bandage (field dressing) to a bleeding limb and apply a seal to a penetrating chest wound. If an infantryman can keep a wounded comrade alive long enough for either Geordie or myself to get to them, the battle will be half won.

Over the years, I have delivered many similar training sessions to bored soldiers who have shown little interest. With the prospect of combat looming, the troops are attentive during the medical training and work hard to get it right. I am pleased.

A day or two later, Phil issues orders for the company's first patrol. It will be a limited foray to some of the closest villages lying to the north of COP Zeebrugge, with the intent of providing reassurance to the local population. Ideally we will demonstrate that we can provide them with security while also gaining information on the enemy's strengths and dispositions in the area.

Geordie is to provide medical support for this patrol, moving at the rear of the company snake (single file deployment) with the CSM's party. The CSM's role is to facilitate rearward evacuation of casualties and forward movement of ammunition and water. Although we are operating in a contested battlespace with a 360-degree threat profile the logistic support concept remains linear, with the understanding that being to the rear of the company snake makes you no less likely to come under enemy attack.

For this first patrol, I remain back at the base to provide medical cover for the troops who have not deployed: the operations room team, the mortar section, those providing base security and the chef, who is busy cooking the next hot meal to be served soon after the company's return. As with the CSM's party, these men are not out on patrol but they can still become wounded. The base could come under attack from mortars, 107-mm rockets or direct-fire weapons such as machine guns, and the chef could accidentally pour boiling water over himself. I decide to camp out in the operations room for the duration of the patrol, which enables me to listen in on the radio net and receive an early warning of any casualties.

For each patrol, Dave remains in the operations room to monitor the progress of the patrol, record events on the big operations map and maintain the flow of communications between Phil's tactical headquarters (Company Tac), the platoons on the ground, the platoon that provides over-watch from the high peaks behind the base and the joint operations centre in Camp Bastion. It is a pleasure to watch Dave perform this role; he clearly relishes what he is doing and goes about his business with a boyish enthusiasm.

The communications kit in the ops room generates

significant heat which, despite the air-conditioning, combines with the rising temperature of the day to turn the operations room into something of a sauna. Early on in the patrol, Dave removes his shirt and lights a cigarette, announcing with a broad grin that this is now officially a smoking area.

The patrol passes without incident and the company returns, having patrolled out for a distance of about three kilometres without sight of anyone, friendly, hostile or neutral. During the patrol, an interpreter has been listening in to Taliban communications traffic using an ICOM scanner. The interpreter tells Dave that the enemy has been observing the company throughout the patrol and provides a running commentary of their observations. Towards the end of the patrol, Phil gives orders for the mortar section to put down a smokescreen to cover the company's extraction.

Outside, in the weapon pits that sit next to my medical facility, the mortar section commander shouts fire mission instructions to his men; there is a frenzy of activity as the correct ammunition nature is selected, the range and elevation set and the figures shouted back in confirmation. Within minutes the mortar line comes alive with a series of deafening reports, echoed a short while later by the distant crump of impacting smoke bombs. I take a wander outside to watch the mortar line in action.

Looking north across the valley, I see several pillars of smoke merge to form a smokescreen which drifts on the gentle breeze. On the nearside of the smokescreen, about 800 metres away, I observe the company strung out over a distance of about one kilometre, making its way back along the road into the village of Tangye to return to base. Twenty minutes later, the last man is home. The first patrol of the tour has been completed without a shot being fired. Next time, it will be a different story.

6 FIRST CASUALTY

In the afternoon following the company's first patrol, one of the men from company headquarters comes to the medical facility with a written warning order which provides me with the outline details of a patrol that will go out the following day. I skim through the details, taking note of the type of operation, equipment required and the times of the O group (briefing) and the patrol itself.

Several hours later, after our evening meal, the officers, CSM and sergeants of C Company and its attached personnel are seated in the briefing area that adjoins the ops room. Phil uses the large ops map to deliver a ground brief and an overview of the general situation before launching into the orders. 10 and 11 platoons, along with the Afghan national army platoon and the Grenadier Guards OMLT, will patrol 2-3 kilometres south of our base to the village of Kajaki Olya.

Phil's intent is twofold; to show our presence, providing confidence to the local population, and to confirm the position of the forward line of enemy troops (FLET). The changeover of units has resulted in a reduction in patrol activity and there is reason to suspect that the Taliban may have taken this opportunity to re-infiltrate positions from which they have previously been dislodged. The patrol will depart at 06.00. Until we have more medical personnel, Geordie and I have agreed to take turns at patrolling with the CSM's party at the back end of the company snake. Pete usually patrols on the CSM's quad bike, which tows a trailer and stretcher for emergency casualty evacuation.

My decision to take part might be viewed as controversial - it appears to fly in the face of the concept of moving casualties from a lower level of care to a higher level of care, and some might take the view that, as a nursing officer, I am too valuable an asset to be placed in harm's way. However, I feel that neither rank nor clinical qualification can justify allowing Geordie to bear the brunt of the rigours and danger of daily patrolling while I sit in the relative safety of the base.

As we file out at the end of the briefing, I pause for a brief chat with the CSM. Among other things, we discuss the matter of ending treatment and resuscitation of men who are killed outright before I can reach them. We agree that, where possible, I will treat the casualty at least until he is in the medical facility, thereby demonstrating to his comrades that all efforts have been made to save his life. The only exception will be if there is clear and undeniable evidence of death.

The following morning, I wake up at 04.15 and go through a final check of my equipment, giving my rifle a quick battle-clean and applying more oil to the working parts. After an early breakfast, the company forms up; once everyone is accounted for, we move out of the back gate to start the patrol. The company patrols down the gravel road that parallels the Helmand river as it meanders through a series of bends down into Kajaki Olya. With a spacing of eight to ten metres between each man, fifteen minutes pass before those of us at the rear move off. With a pounding heart, I walk out of the back gate on my first foot patrol of the tour.

It takes a long time to reach Kajaki Olya as the company halts every few hundred metres. Each time we stop, I drop down into a kneeling fire position, the weight of my body armour and equipment transferring through my right knee. The kneepads I've been issued make the discomfort more tolerable, but it isn't long before I need to shift position to ease the pins and needles in my foot. When I get up to start walking again, I have to give my legs a shake to get moving, no longer the young man I used to be.

After an hour of start-stop patrolling, we move into the northern fringes of Kajaki Olya. Descending into the village, I can discern an inestimable number of mud-walled compounds and houses stretching the eight hundred or so metres that run downhill to the river on my right and a couple of kilometres down the valley. To the left of the road, a smaller but still considerable number of compounds clusters the uphill slope for about three hundred metres until the ground becomes too steep to have been built upon.

Aside from bearing the visible scars of a quarter-century of conflict and the vestiges of once-functional electricity and telephone lines, I imagine that this scene must have changed very little in the last couple of hundred years. As we move into the village, our view of the world is restricted by the houses that we pass. The observation posts on the craggy peaks behind us are able to see in depth, but their view is also limited. The enemy could be on the other side of a wall and we would have no idea.

We haven't been in the village very long when a burst of machine-gun fire passes over our heads with an angry snapping sound, followed seconds later by a corresponding series of thumps from the observation posts on the high ground behind us. The snapping is the noise of the bullets passing overhead; the thumping is the delayed report from the weapon actually being fired. Sitting astride his quad bike which he's parked in the cover of a wall, Pete tells us that the observation posts were firing warning shots to persuade a suspected dicker (enemy observer) to pack up his kit and take the rest of the day off. The burst of .50-calibre heavy machine-gun fire has apparently had the desired effect.

As the company probes further into the village, we hear over the radio that the interpreters listening to enemy chat are reporting that the Taliban can see us and are preparing to send in suicide bombers. Soon after, while we are static at a crossroads in the village, there is a tense moment when an old man comes walking through leading a donkey laden with pannier baskets. In a conflict that has seen the Taliban use all manner of ruses to mount attacks on coalition forces, a donkey-borne bomb is not beyond the realms of possibility.

As the lead platoons are clearing the village, Pete notifies me of my first casualty of the tour – a Royal Engineers sapper has been hit in the hand by a swinging metal door while moving through a building. He has lost most of his fingernail and a chunk of tissue has been gouged away. I apply a quick dressing and Pete arranges for the injured man to be taken back to the base where I will treat him on my return from patrol.

A short while later the company is reaching the limit of exploitation, a pre-designated point at which it will stop moving, hold the ground for a short period and observe the pattern of life before making an orderly and balanced withdrawal to the base. This conflict is not about winning ground or killing the enemy, it is about winning people. Some of the people will support us, some will be irreconcilable whilst others will be undecided; these last are the people whom we need to convince. In a country that has seen armies come and go since the time of Genghis Khan, one can assume that the undecided will be hedging their bets for some time. As we were told in our training, we have the watches but the Taliban have the time.

As the troops at the front end of the company complete their clearance of the final compound, the morning calm is shattered by a storm of small arms fire and rocket-propelled grenades. Along with Pete and the rest of the CSM's party, I am crouching behind a low wall on a flat roof watching the firefight unfold. There is not much to see, but plenty to hear; the distinctive rattle of AK fire being answered by the a rippling volley of fire from our own rifles, swelling to a crescendo with staccato bursts from the Minimi light machine guns and the deeper roar of a general purpose machine gun.

Our opening performance of the tour is completed by the heavy percussion of the 81-mm mortars at our base which make a repetitive crump on impact and the deep thumping sound of the .50-calibre machine guns pouring fire on the enemy from the peaks. It is not long before Alex, our joint terminal attack controller (JTAC), has a United States air force F16E on station to bring some real firepower to bear. We have a grandstand view as the fast jet roars in at low level to make two successive strafing runs on the enemy positions.

In the meantime, Phil has given orders over the radio to use the aggressive overmatch that we have achieved as breathing space to conduct the planned extraction. Climbing down from the roof, we set off at a steady jog, retracing our route back up the main road to one of our previous locations. Pete tells us that the Taliban can be heard on the scanner defiantly telling their commanders that they are still alive in spite of the mortars and strafing. As we start walking back up the valley, there is more (ineffective) small arms fire coming from behind us.

We now have more air support on station and the valley reverberates to the deafening impact of 500-pound bombs. Seconds later, we hear another burst of AK fire from the compound that has just been bombed. I am amazed and despondent that these guys are still firing in spite of the ordnance that has just been dropped on their heads.

However, word comes down the line that our previously defiant Taliban friend is now crying to his boss because four of his friends are dead and that he needs a doctor and some bandages.

After the tiring walk back up the hill to our base, we can relax and unwind a little. I have completed my first patrol in Afghanistan but more importantly, C Company has come through its first contact with the enemy unscathed.

Back at combat outpost Zeebrugge, I have some work to do. The Royal Engineer with the hand injury is waiting for me. After giving him a local anaesthetic, I remove what is left of his fingernail, clean up the wound and dress it before giving him some pain killers and antibiotics. As he has a reduced range of movement in the injured fingers, I make arrangements for him to go back to Camp Bastion for treatment at the hospital as soon as possible.

We spend the rest of the day on post-patrol administration and rest until the officers and seniors come together in the evening for Phil's daily briefing. The mood is quite jovial, with everyone's morale buoyed by the successful patrol. I hope that this is the beginning of a long run of luck, but deep down I know it is only a matter of time before I will be required to treat more serious casualties.

In the days following C Company's successful first brush with the enemy, Phil maintains the momentum of patrol activity. I imagine that the general idea is to keep the Taliban on the back foot and reinforce the success of that first small victory. Geordie and I continue to take turns at patrolling with the troops and I discover that I am more anxious when I am left back in camp than when I am out on the ground. From the moment the company moves out until the time that the last man steps back into the base, I strut and fret between my medical facility and the operations room, anxious to keep abreast of developments with the patrol.

Several patrols pass where the enemy activity consists of nothing more than sporadic rifle fire, which is met with return fire and a supporting mortar fire mission in response. The mercury is starting to hit one hundred degrees on a daily basis, and Geordie and I find ourselves treating a small number of soldiers for heat illness after each patrol.

In between dealing with patients and patrolling, we also have some administrative duties to attend to. We do our best to keep the medical facility in a clean and tidy state by sweeping the floor and damp-dusting the surfaces daily. Unfortunately, no matter how hard we try, a fine film of sandy dust penetrates everywhere. Twice a week, I am required to phone through to our headquarters in Camp Bastion to provide an operational update, request medical resupply and notify medical ops of the number and type of patients we have treated. Every week I conduct a full check of all controlled medications, and every day emergency items such as the oxygen and suction are examined. There is also an opportunity for some downtime, during which I read and listen to music on my personal CD player; we sometimes watch movies on Geordie's laptop.

My little family in the medical centre soon grows with the arrival of Joe and Steve, who make up the military police detachment. I have an immediate affinity for Joe, as we are from the same part of south London. Joe is a likeable, cheeky chap with a tendency to make light of life. One evening, just before we go to bed, Joe reports that he can see two shapes moving stealthily from left to right about fifty metres behind the back fence of the base. Geordie notifies the ops room and the quick reaction force is deployed, while the mortar line is tasked with firing illumination flares into the night sky above us.

While this is happening, Geordie, the military policemen and I sit behind the medical facility with our rifles scanning the middle distance. The report of mortar fire fills the air, shortly followed by the distinctive pops of the flares detaching from the bomb case. Suspended from small parachutes, they spiral gracefully to earth, the white hot phosphorous guttering as it burns; this casts shadows that flicker eerily across the hillside until it finally burns out about thirty metres from the ground, leaving only a vestige of a smoke trail to indicate that it was ever there. Between the illum. and the QRF's night vision equipment, no movement is detected. The most likely explanation is that the moving shapes were animals of some description, probably jackals.

Later that week, following a day without patrols, we are woken in the small hours of the morning by a brief, high-pitched whoosh that is followed instantly by an explosive impact; the unmistakable sound of a 107-mm rocket. The firing point is identified as a topographic feature known as Nipple Hill. By a stroke of luck, there is a combat air patrol in the vicinity and when our JTAC calls in a fire mission, the United States air force kindly drops a couple of 1000-lb bombs on the heads of those who sought to disturb our beauty sleep.

The following morning, I am up early for a patrol to Shebaz Kheyll, a village to the north. We haven't got far and are still making our way through Tangye when the CSM notifies me that the fire support group vehicles have been fired upon from enemy positions to the north. Within a few minutes, Pete tells me that we have a casualty to deal with.

Moving into Tangye at a steady jog, we take up position at the Afghan national auxiliary police station and the sergeant-major rides forward on his quad bike to retrieve the casualty. There are still no specific details, so I hunker down and start preparing some medical kit that I think I might need.

While I am waiting for the casualty to be brought to me, without my knowledge the Pinzgauer truck has been dispatched from the base with Geordie on board. What happens next is still a mystery to me, but apparently the Pinzgauer came head to head with the company sergeant-major, who was returning from the contact area with the casualty. Pete urged the Pinzgauer driver to turn around and 'get the fuck out of Dodge' as there was lots of incoming fire.

In the meantime, I have been directed to move locations, so we are now in a situation where I don't know where the casualty is and the sergeant-major doesn't know where I am. When I finally catch up with Pete, I discover that the casualty has received initial treatment, been loaded onto the Pinzgauer and is on his way to the medical facility with Geordie. The MERT helicopter has been dispatched.

Phil decides to pull the plug on the patrol, but not before calling in an airstrike on the location from which the fire support group was engaged. A pair of fast jets swoops down, dropping a series of bombs which cause the hilltop to erupt in a cloud of flame, dirt and debris.

The casualty, a young .50-calibre gunner from the fire support group has been hit in the groin by a 7.62-mm AK bullet. Miraculously, there is no damage to major vessels or bones and he undergoes surgery at Camp Bastion within two hours of being wounded. It is not a milestone to be celebrated. Although he was very lucky, this young man –

a reservist university student who volunteered for the tour - is the company's first casualty. Within a few hours, his friends have posted a sign on the entrance to their accommodation. It reads: **.50-cal gunner wanted, must have own body armour – apply within.**

During these early days of the tour, life in Zeebrugge takes on a pace of its own. On days without patrols, I rise at around 06.00 and take time to sort out my personal admin. This sort of routine is ingrained in anyone who has ever served in the armed forces. The top priority is to clean my rifle and the second priority is to sort out my personal equipment; washing and shaving takes third place. As a medical team, we have to add the checking of our medical equipment to this list, ensuring that the emergency kit in our treatment bay is serviceable and that all medications are in date. I also have to account for the narcotics with which we have been issued and, together with Geordie, do the damp-dusting, sweeping and mopping.

Once the morning routine is completed, I hold the morning sick parade, at which any soldiers requiring routine treatment for illnesses and minor injuries present themselves. During my time at Zeebrugge, I'm faced with a broad range of ailments: these include boils and abscesses in embarrassing places, haemorrhoids, diarrhoea, a sexually-transmitted infection, and an episode of acute (but thankfully mild) psychosis caused by the anti-malarial drug Mefloquine, which was given to most of the men from C Company as chemo-prophylaxis while on pre-deployment training in Kenya.

One morning, a young soldier reports sick with an acute infection caused by an impacted wisdom tooth. I give the man some pain-killers and discuss his case with the dental team in Camp Bastion. They recommend starting a course of antibiotics and sending him back for assessment and treatment. I have just started making arrangements through the ops room when the sergeant-major comes to see me. Pete tells me that the man with dental problems is his worst soldier and that he believes he is malingering. This presents me with a dilemma; the errant soldier has a genuine dental problem, but I place a high value on the opinion of C Company's senior soldier. Despite Pete's protestations, I send the man back to Camp Bastion with a referral letter to the senior dental officer. When I phone the dental centre at Camp Bastion a couple of days later, I'm disappointed to learn that the soldier has not booked in. Pete later tells me that the soldier went straight to the chaplain and cried off operations. He doesn't return to the company. I am angry that the soldier hoodwinked me, but satisfied that I did the right thing.

Once the morning routine is done, there is considerable time to kill. A satellite phone enables us to telephone our families back home and, as the tour goes on, we are given access to the internet and a SMS machine. Although this helps to dull the pain of separation from loved ones, the contrast between our austere, simple and violent existence and the banal complexity of family life with an absentee parent is marked. When I do phone home, I find that the conversations are sometimes stilted due to my inability to 'be there' and my reluctance to reveal the extent to which I'm in the thick of the action.

In the ops briefings, we often refer to the northern FLET (forward line of enemy troops) and the southern FLET. In reality, there is only one FLET and it encircles us. Because the area of operations is bisected by the Helmand river and our eastern flank is shielded by the high ground, our movement is channelled into two main mobility corridors: north and south. Throughout our time in Kajaki, Phil constantly switches our efforts between the two areas to ensure that we keep the enemy at arm's length from the key location of the Kajaki dam and power station which, if fully renovated, could provide power to the whole of Helmand province. Since the wounding of the .50-calibre machine gunner in Tangye, we have maintained our focus on the villages to the north. On our next patrol, we are heading south.

The aims of the patrol are simple and more or less a repeat of our previous ones - Clear, Find, Defeat, Reassure. Our job is to move back into Kajaki Olya, clear the village, find any enemy and defeat them, thereby reassuring any local civilians that the Afghan government is providing them with security and that NATO forces have the ability and willingness to take on the Taliban. This tactic is known as 'cutting the grass'. The idea is that each of the District Centres forms the centre point of an 'ink spot' in which the defeating the enemy is not an end in itself, but instead provides the means of creating a space in which stability and good governance can flourish. As the campaign progresses, each of these ink spots is supposed to expand as the government's sphere of influence expands until all the ink spots join up. The ultimate aim in Kajaki is for the hydroelectric power plant at the dam to be restored, which has the potential to provide power throughout Helmand and transform people's lives for the better. Before this can happen, ISAF needs to have better control of districts further south in the Sangin Valley. Throughout the summer, a number of big operations will take place to try to achieve this. One day until it will be the time for a large scale operation in Kajaki, until then, we just have to keep cutting the grass, showing the Taliban who is in charge, keep them a safe distance from the hydroelectric dam and try to convince the locals that they will be better provided for by the Government than the Taliban.

Once again I am to patrol with the CSM's party; the main difference is timing. This time we are moving off late in the morning. As we step off, I am staggered at the intensity of the heat to which we are exposed. Radiating directly from the sun and also reflected from the ground beneath our feet, it is nigh-intolerable. When we come to a standstill, it is impossible to remain in one position for too long because whichever body parts are in contact with the ground soon begin to cook – bum, feet, knees. I take to switching position every minute or so.

Although we manage to push further into Kajaki Olya than on the last patrol, it is not long before the Taliban initiates contact by opening fire on the lead platoon. Just before the shooting starts, a group of us climb onto a compound roof to try to get eyes on the enemy, which means that we have a good view of the fighting. The men up front are engaged in a savage firefight with the Taliban, who in turn are throwing back everything they have. In the distance, frustratingly out of the range of our weapons, I see a number of black-robed figures who appear to be directing the hostile activities. In the middle distance, our unseen enemy's position is betrayed by the tell-tale grey-white smoke trails of rocket-propelled grenades which arc gracefully, almost lazily, over the compound walls.

The quiet of the day has been replaced by the rattle and crack of small-arms fire. Every now and then, we flinch and duck as stray bullets snap over our heads or whiz in between us like angry metal wasps. Once the TIC (troops in contact) has been declared open on the radio net, Phil is able to request additional fire support through JTAC Alex. Alex, call sign 'Widow 83', is a youthful sergeant from the Royal Artillery who has the joy of carrying a big radio with him wherever he goes. This radio, complete with a dish-shaped antenna, gives Alex the power to speak directly with the fast jet pilots, guiding them onto the enemy targets. The TIC has been open for about ten minutes when Pete, listening on his radio, relays the message from

Phil that an airstrike will occur in ninety seconds.

To begin with, the noise of the fast jet's engines is almost imperceptible above the din of the battle. As the seconds tick by, the aircraft noise builds to a crescendo while the pilot circles the area searching for his target. Pete calls out again, telling us that the strike will be in thirty seconds. Looking on with a mounting sense of anticipation, time seems almost to come to a standstill. The forward sections of the lead platoon have popped green smoke grenades to indicate their positions to the plane. A message comes down from Pete, telling us that the strike is imminent.

The words have barely left Pete's mouth when a menacing shadow swoops from the sky accompanied by the roar of thirty-millimetre cannon strafing the Taliban positions. The fast jet climbs high into the sky, making a corkscrew turn as it ascends before banking right to break out of the climb and coming back round for another run, this time unleashing a pair of thousand-pound bombs. A succession of orange fireballs flicker momentarily across the enemy positions as the bombs explode before transforming into burgeoning pillars of smoke and debris which are sucked into the air. An instant later the crash of the impact reaches us, accompanied by a rumble that causes our rooftop vantage point to shudder, reminding me of the time I experienced an earth tremor in California.

Despite the best efforts of the pilot, the enemy are still firing. I am surprised to hear a lance corporal quoting Shakespeare: "Full of sound and fury, signifying nothing," he comments. I reply that I believe Kipling would be more appropriate, reciting, 'When you're wounded and left on Afghanistan's plains'. It turns out that this soldier is a reservist and is patrolling with the CSM's party today because he has a knee injury which affects his ability to fight with his section.

The firefight continues with our guys having the upper hand, effectively suppressing the enemy, while the fast jet makes more attack runs. When the fast jet pilot goes off station, his place is taken by well-controlled indirect fire from the mortar line back at Zeebrugge. The fire support group has also deployed and is providing additional suppressive fire with the heavy machine guns and grenade machine guns mounted on their WMIK Land Rovers.

When Phil decides to break contact, it is done in an orderly manner with the platoons echeloning through each other so that there is always a significant amount of weaponry aimed at the enemy. As I walk out of Kajaki Olya towards Route 611, I turn back to see plumes of smoke still billowing from the enemy positions in a line of compounds. There is no small arms fire now.

As we make our way back, it becomes apparent that the Shakespearian lance corporal is having problems with his knee, hobbling and limping, but refusing all offers of help. We are moving up a broad alleyway with our backs to the enemy when he collapses on all fours, moaning with pain. When I try to help him stand he gets stroppy, pushing me away. This riles me; the alleyway is wide and occupies a reverse slope – a sniper's dream – and this clown has decided to have a temper tantrum in full view of the enemy. Not only is it embarrassing to witness, his action is also compromising the safety of the three or four men, myself included, who have stopped to try to help him. I'm torn between my professional concern for his wellbeing and the desire to give him a kick up the arse. Fortunately Pete appears and has some stern words with the man before taking him back to Zeebrugge on the quad bike trailer. I'm relieved to be off the reverse slope but find it hard to be forgiving towards the injured man.

We return to Zeebrugge retracing our outbound route, an

uphill trudge in the blistering heat. I have sucked my water bladder almost dry and fatigue hits me almost as soon as we're back through the gates of the base. Before I can do any post-patrol admin, I have to assess 'knee man'. He has a long standing injury and should never have been deployed into a rifle platoon. To use the technical term, his knee is 'proper broken'. I give him some anti-inflammatories and pain-killers, make the necessary phone calls and write a referral letter to get him reviewed with a recommendation for rest and physiotherapy in Camp Bastion.

After rifle cleaning, kit replenishment, rehydration and shower, I get the chance to speak with squadron headquarters in Camp Bastion. My squadron commander has some welcome news for me. I am getting some additional medics to bolster the team. This means I will be able to have a medic up on the peaks with the platoon that mans the observation posts.

7 CLEARING CHINEH

Evening time in Kajaki: the setting sun casts an orange glow across the mountain tops behind the camp as I take the short walk across to the ops room for the evening brief. Approaching the entrance, I say a quick hello to Dave, who is standing outside smoking with some of the boys. The platoon commanders, Tom, Manie and Sam, along with their sergeants, have the honour of sitting on the front two rows of bench seats. Howard, the Grenadier Guards OMLT commander also sits up front with his colour sergeant. The rest of us sit in the cheap seats or stand, a motley array of supporting actors: Tom, the artillery fire support team commander, Mark, the fire support group commander, Shane from mortars, Alice, the Royal Engineers commander, Peter, the liaison officer and me – med.

Everyone is in a good mood. The company conducted an uneventful patrol this morning and this afternoon a helicopter has dropped off supplies, mail and a handful of reinforcements; these include Matt, the company medic, who is a welcome addition to my thinly-spread team. Phil enters the room followed by Pete, who stands off to one side while Phil gives us the heads-up on the next day's patrol. We are now familiar with the ground, so Phil doesn't give us a detailed orientation, instead jumping straight to the intelligence brief and the orders for tomorrow's patrol. It is my turn to go out this time and I'm filled with a sense of excitement at the news that we will be taking another jaunt into Kajaki Olya, this time pushing further down into the town and towards the river. Almost every time we go south to Kajaki Olya, we mix things up a bit and have a good fight. Aside from the wounded machine-gunner, the company has sustained no battle casualties and seems to be leading a blessed existence.

By the time I return to the medical facility, night has fallen and it is pitch black. I get the guys together to let them know our part in Phil's plan, which is pretty much the same as all the other patrols. Matt and Geordie will stay in camp, I will patrol with the CSM's party.

The briefing completed, I prep my kit for patrol and join the men for a spot of evening entertainment. One of the military policemen has received his laptop and DVD stash in today's supply drop, so we are able to spend the evening watching a couple of movies. I have a bit of a chat with Matt to get to know him a little better. At first look he seems to know his stuff, but only time will tell if he is truly on top of his game.

In the morning, we have the luxury of a lie-in as the patrol does not go out until 11.00. It is still April, but the heat seems more intense each day - of course we do not help ourselves by wearing body armour and helmets. So far I am coping with the heat, but I perspire so heavily that I come back from patrols feeling decidedly soggy. I have decided to ditch some of the extra pouches that attach to the front of my body armour as they get in the way when I'm scrambling over rooftops and climbing over walls in the deserted towns and villages interspersed across our area of operations.

It takes about twenty minutes for the company to shake out and leave the back gate. As usual, I will be at the back of the snake for the duration of the patrol. I always feel that this is great for the route out, when the point platoon is heading toward the enemy positions, but not so good for the return trip when I am closest to the enemy and have my back towards them for much of the time. Somehow, the prospect of being shot in the arse is less appealing than taking a bullet head-on.

The route out is taken at a painstakingly slow pace while the lads on point clear their way through, compound by compound, mindful of the fact that the enemy may well have left an IED or mine to inflict casualties and hinder our progress. It takes about an hour to cover the first kilometre; start-stop-up-down, all the time tormented by the bright ball of flame in the sky that slowly broils us inside our Kevlar ovens. We finally get going and it is a relief to be moving again. A light breeze blows gently uphill from the Helmand river, which cools us off a little despite its slight warmth. This is no time to relax, however, as the message soon comes across the radio net that the ICOM scanner is picking up lots of enemy chatter which indicates that they have seen us and are preparing a nasty surprise.

As we penetrate further into the town, we have to do quite a bit of running to cover the open ground between houses and compound walls; one man moving, the next man covering the likely direction of enemy threat with his weapon before another man takes his place and he makes the dash of death himself. As we move down a track in between settlements, the scenery becomes more verdant, almost picturesque; poppies grow waist high, their heavy heads bobbing lazily back and forth in the breeze and nearby, an unseen brook babbles gently downhill towards the river.

We soon find ourselves in the compound that was bombed during our last patrol into Kajaki Olya. The wall has collapsed at the end closest to us and we scramble over it to gain access. Once inside, we wait for the platoons to move towards their final objectives. Pete tells us to that we will be staying put here for the time being. As we are all beginning to overheat, we post a sentry and take the opportunity to get into some hard cover and remove our helmets.

I sit and chat with Steve. He is 10 Platoon's sergeant, a likeable man who leads his young soldiers with the gentle firmness of an older brother. As Steve's platoon is currently manning the observation posts in the peaks, he has taken the opportunity to come out on this patrol as part of the company sergeant-major's party to familiarize himself with the ground. When I mention that today is my son's first birthday, Steve expresses genuine sympathy for my being here and not at home.

After about thirty minutes, one of the lead platoons comes under sustained attack with a heavy rate of fire reinforced by a couple of rocket-propelled grenades. Both of these whizz over our heads, coming a little too close for comfort. The company responds to the enemy fire in kind. To our front, unseen, the rattle of small-arms fire indicates that the forward platoon has begun the task of suppressing the enemy, while behind us, battle is joined by the heavy weapons of the fire support group and salvos of mortar fire from Zeebrugge. An outgoing missile whooshes over - a Javelin, fired by one of Steve's men up in the peaks – impacting with a boom somewhere to our front.

Following this, the enemy fire dies down, evidence that the company is winning the firefight. Word comes down that we have an American fast jet on station. The pilot makes a few low passes to keep the enemy's head down, but he does not need to drop any ordnance. A short while later, it is clear that the Taliban are not in the mood for a big fight today and Phil decides to break contact and withdraw. People are getting low on water, the afternoon is wearing on and the Taliban ICOM chatter claims to have us surrounded.

We extract back to Zeebrugge without event, but my day is

not done. First, I have to treat a couple of men suffering with mild heat illness and dehydration and another with a knee problem. I assess my patients, prescribing each of them some medication before heading across to the de-briefing; here we discover that, far from having us surrounded, we actually had the enemy surrounded, offering an explanation for the Taliban's uncharacteristic hesitance. Sitting in the debriefing, I wonder if we haven't just missed an opportunity to deliver a decisive blow to the enemy in Kajaki Olya, but the platoons had each achieved their objectives and there is always a possibility that by pushing on, the company would have been made vulnerable by its own offensive action; a well-coordinated counter-attack into our flanks or rear (something that the Taliban will always try) could have resulted in the isolation and loss of a platoon or section. On balance, I feel that Phil made the right call.

After the de-briefing, I get the chance to phone home and have some baby-talk with my boy. It is not the most riveting conversation in history, but it is one that I would not miss for the world. As I finish the call, I am overwhelmed with sadness at having spent my baby boy's first birthday being shot at by total strangers in a bombed-out compound in an obscure corner of a distant land.

The next few days pass relatively quietly for C Company. A couple of routine patrols are mounted, one to secure the helicopter landing site for supply drop by helicopter and another to an outlying village that we have not visited before. The purpose of the latter patrol is to confirm that it is inhabited, reassure those living there and show the flag.

Geordie goes on this second patrol while I stay in camp and pass a fretful couple of hours waiting and worrying, hoping for the safe return of the patrol. I spend some of the time sitting with Dave in the operations room to keep tabs on the company's progress. It is always a relief to hear the commanders radioing in to report that they have crossed the bridge near Tangye, indicating that they are back in the comparative safety of COP Zeebrugge.

Sadly, the same cannot be said of the other companies in the Vikings battlegroup. On 13 April, the buzz goes around that A Company, based at the outpost of Now Zad, has come under sustained contact from multiple firing points and has suffered a soldier killed in action. Phil confirms the news at the evening briefing. The casualty is named as Private Chris Gray, a nineteen-year-old from Leicestershire. This sad news reinforces to me how fortunate C Company has been so far. Most of our patrols have resulted in contact with the enemy and we have had only one serious casualty, who is reported to be making good progress.

Private Gray is the first fatality of the tour and I'm hit by mixed emotions. As a parent, I feel a deep sense of sympathy for the bereaved family. We have only been in Afghanistan for a few weeks and, if it has not happened already, that soldier's parents will soon have a knock on the door from a stranger who must give them the news they have dreaded since the moment they waved him goodbye.

As a soldier, I want us to go out and get some payback. As a professional nurse, I resolve to myself that I will fight hard for the life of every wounded man who passes through my hands. I fear that I am not equal to such an onerous task and pray that in the midst of the tumult, God will grant me courage, calmness, clarity of thought and presence of mind to do my job well when I am called on to do so.

It may be that God will have to deliver on my prayer sooner rather than later; the company is due to conduct a deliberate clearance operation in the village of Chineh, which sits on the western edge of the M1 wadi, on the northern side of the area of operations. Phil warns us to expect casualties.

On the night of 15 April, Phil delivers a full set of orders for the patrol into Chineh, which will commence at dark o'clock the following morning. I have received another welcome addition to the medical team; Ricky, a sergeant, has been sent as a dedicated medic for the Afghan platoon and their OMLT advisors. The plan is simple - move out to a rendezvous point, from which Phil will mount a clearance of compounds and dwellings by leapfrogging platoons through each other. That way, two platoons will provide support to the platoon conducting the clearance. The fire support group will deploy to a flank to provide heavy weapon support against depth positions.

We also have the usual support from the mortar section in camp, the heavy machine guns and the Javelin rocket launchers on the peaks which will be augmented by dedicated air support in the form of a pair of Apache attack helicopters and a US air force B-2 bomber. With the growth of my medical team, I am in a position to provide a more sophisticated medical plan. Matt and I will patrol with the company sergeant-major's party, Ricky will be forward-based on the Pinzgauer support vehicle and Geordie will remain in camp to assist with the coordination of the evacuation, should it be required.

After Phil's orders, I return to the medical facility and back-brief my team, after which we settle into the routine of prepping our equipment and getting some rest. We have had a couple of days without patrol and I find that I am wakeful and keyed up when I should be getting some rest.

Private Gray's death has served as a reminder that we are playing a serious game out here. We are due to move off well before dawn and have a suitably early reveille to ensure that we cross the start line in good order and on time.

I have slept for only a few hours when I rise and get dressed. There is no need to wake the troops; one by one they all get up, pulling on boots and combat uniforms. A short while later, Ricky joins us and those of us going out on the ground don body armour, webbing and helmets. I run through a couple of final checks: jumping up and down to make sure that I do not rattle or clank, squirting a dash of oil onto the working parts of my rifle and fitting a magazine of thirty rounds to it. I am ready to go.

We leave the medical facility to meet up with the commanders of the call-signs with which we will patrol. Matt and I greet Pete, his location in the pitch black given away by the purr of his quad bike ticking over, whilst Ricky lingers by the Pinzgauer to await the arrival of the driver and commander. Once all of the formalities of filling out flap sheets (a list of the men deploying on the ground) have been completed, the company moves off.

Our route takes us down the hill, through the wrought-iron gate that marks the end of guaranteed friendly territory and out into bandit country. Crossing the wooden bridge in the dark, I tread carefully to avoid falling through the large holes in the causeway. To do so would mean certain death, either from the crashing cataract of water that gushes down the waterfall adjacent to the dam or at the hands of the enemy, should one be hapless enough to be washed downstream into Kajaki Olya or Kajaki Sofla.

Every man in C Company knows the story of Russia

House, the abandoned building on our base which was reportedly the scene of the butchering of a number of Soviet conscripts, and we know this much - a quick death in combat would be preferable to slow torture and mutilation at the hands of the Taliban. Safely across the river, we move through Tangye village and cross the M1 wadi at the end closest to our base.

As I make my way along the track, I am almost bowled off my feet by a small, lolloping black shadow which hurtles and weaves between the wraith-like forms of the patrolling soldiers. Tangye the dog, a beautiful, stocky black labrador has joined us for the patrol. Tangye was found abandoned by our Royal Marines predecessors in the village whose name he bears. Loved by the soldiers, the dog serves as a talisman on our patrols. We know from the ICOM chatter that the Taliban do not like him, thinking him to be a mine-detecting dog. Whenever Tangye joins us on a patrol the Taliban do their damnedest to kill him, but he has more lives than a cat and always comes through unscathed.

As we approach the base of Shrine hill, the company comes to a halt and adopts a temporary defensive posture. This is the final rendezvous point before the platoons move in to start the clearance of Chineh. As the first glimmers of daylight emerge, I pack away my night-vision kit and survey the scene before me: the best part of two hundred men are gathered here in an attempt to seriously ruin someone's day. I cast my mind back to the epic Anglo-Saxon poem 'The Battle of Maldon' and ruminate that C (Essex) Company could well be considered to be the direct descendants of Byrhtnoth's Army:

> *'He rode up and counselled them - his soldiers he taught*
> *How they should stand, and their standing to keep,*
> *And bade them their round shields rightly to hold*
> *Fast to their forearms, that they flinch not at all.'*

The intervening eleven hundred years might have seen huge advances in weapon technology, but there are some aspects of combat that will endure for as long as it remains a human activity: the pre-climactic rise in tension, the steeling of nerves and the banishment of fear to the deepest recesses of one's mind.

As the sun begins to rise, Phil decides to kick-start the operation to avoid the company being ambushed in the open while standing out like the proverbial bulldog's bollocks. As the men move off, using a kilometre-long strip of woodland as cover, the company sergeant-major's party remains a tactical bound behind, taking cover among the trees and bushes.

By the time we are in position, the sun has risen and it's only a matter of time before the fighting starts. Phil has sent a message through JTAC Alex instructing the waiting air support to remain over the horizon until the company comes into contact with the enemy. Once Phil declares that the TIC is open, he can pour fire onto the Taliban from both ground and air. We don't have long to wait.

The village of Chineh must have existed for hundreds of years. It is a higgledy-piggledy array of dun-coloured mud-walled compounds stretching for several hundred metres. It must be cleared room by room, house by house, alleyway by alleyway.

Waking up to discover that we are on their turf, the Taliban open fire with the usual volley of rocket-propelled grenade and small-arms fire. To the north of Chineh is a large hump-backed hill which vaguely resembles a pyramid; with all the imagination that the military can bring to bear, this is known as Pyramid Hill. We now discover that Pyramid Hill is home to a substantial number of Taliban in dug-in positions. We know this because they are whacking the lead platoons with machine-gun fire and a recoilless rifle.

Once battle is joined, the ICOM chatter comes alive and Pete relays to us a running commentary provided by the interpreter. It is the usual talk of 'send reinforcements', 'we have them surrounded', 'get the big thing' (presumably a heavy weapon) and 'send in the suicide bombers', etc. It is all talk that we have heard before, and I suspect that this may be mere nonsense that they make up for our benefit while having a laugh at our expense.

Our position at the strip wood is hardly a vantage point - I cannot really see the battle, but I can certainly hear it. Although we are relatively safe, there is an unnerving moment when the branches of the trees above us start to disintegrate, accompanied by the insistent snapping of bullets and the fizzing sound of a rocket-propelled grenade passing by close over our heads. Somewhere, someone is trying to kill us. Fortunately, they are not making a very good job of it.

As the firefight develops, it seems that anyone in the neighbourhood who owns an AK47 has decided to come and have a pop at us. We are taking fire from Pyramid Hill, the northern end of Chineh, Khovalehebad to our north and Barikju to our east. Phil decides that enough is enough; it is time to let slip the dogs of war and unleash some airpower. The B2 is first to be cued up, dropping bombs onto Pyramid Hill. A shadow flits across the landscape as the pilot makes his run.

The bombs hit their target, the orange flicker of the explosion engulfing the hilltop, followed a split-second later by the sound of a thousand roof slates crashing onto a marble floor as a column of thick black smoke and dust climbs into the sky. This keeps the enemy's heads down and allows the Apache attack helicopters to come in. Compared to the screaming fury of the jet aircraft, the Apache pair seem to move slowly and menacingly toward their quarry, hosing down the enemy with their thirty-millimetre chain guns and the occasional Hellfire missile. Once the enemy has been suppressed the air support backs off, leaving the platoons to carry on their clearance. The ICOM chatter is not so confident now and it is clear that we have given the Taliban a bloody nose.

Surprisingly, though, there is still resistance from the depth positions in the outlying villages and one or two persistent fighters up on Pyramid Hill. Phil decides to break contact and starts the orderly withdrawal of his platoons. As the platoons march back through the strip wood, the B2 drops another bomb onto Pyramid Hill. There is silence for about thirty seconds before the sound of a lone AK is heard firing in impotent anger in our general direction. We figure that if the guy can survive that amount of ordnance being dropped on his head, he probably deserves to live.

The morning's fight is concluded with a combination of smoke and high explosive ordnance being fired by the mortar section, a few suppressive bursts of .50-calibre machine-gun fire and a Javelin missile being fired at a group of enemy who are contemplating the launch of a counter-attack. As the last man in the rear platoon passes our position, we peel off and join the column for the three kilometre walk back to COP Zeebrugge. Crossing the M1 wadi, I meet the Pinzgauer with Ricky on board. As we exchange pleasantries, I observe that Ricky seems to have enjoyed the morning's show.

The worst part about returning from patrol is the two hundred metres of steeply-inclined tarmac road that we have to drag ourselves up to return to base at the very end of the patrol. As I trudge uphill, Pete passes us on the quad bike. For a moment, the temptation to thumb a lift is overpowering, but the soldiers will never have the privilege of asking, so I must not. Geordie is waiting at the top of the hill and is pleased to see the company back home, safe and sound. He passes me the message that there will be a de-briefing in an hour, followed by breakfast. This gives me an hour to clean my rifle and sort out my kit before grabbing a shower.

There are no proper showers in COP Zeebrugge. The only facilities are shower bags (a large neoprene bag with a tube, clamp and watering-can spout at one end and a hook at the other) and a long rail from which to suspend them. The floor of the shower area is built from black plastic roller-track flooring. A successful shower relies on good planning. First, you must fill your shower bag with cold water and leave it out in the early morning sun for a couple of hours. Second, you must make sure you don't leave the bag out too long, to avoid the water being unbearably hot. Third, you must take your shower before the heat of the day is too intense, otherwise you will find yourself doing a bit of a tap dance on floor tiles that are just too hot to stand on. Forget the first and you merely get a cold shower; get the other two wrong and you are in a world of pain. Trust me, it's the kind of mistake you will make only once.

The final thing to bear in mind is that there is practically no privacy; the chances are you will not be showering alone, and today is no exception. As I am soaping up, I am joined by three or four other men. This is not prison, so there is no need to fear dropping one's soap and there is usually a bit of chat and banter. Where one rests one's eyes is important; nobody - especially the company's nursing officer - wants to be accused of being a cock-watcher!
The amount of time you spend showering is limited to the volume of water in the shower bag, so we adopt a ships'

routine – allowing the water to flow only when getting wet and rinsing off. Conserving water in this way ensures that I have some water left over to hand-wash my dirty uniform from the morning's patrol.

At the appointed time, I assemble with the other commanders for the de-briefing. When we are not on patrol, we wear a mixed bag of relaxed dress, mainly running shorts and T-shirts. For the de-briefing we are slightly more formally dressed, most opting for the issued combat shorts and a military T-shirt. Phil gives us a run-through of the patrol and draws out any pertinent learning points and guidance for future operations. The battle damage assessment indicates that the morning's work has resulted in two confirmed enemy dead and an estimation that, based on the ICOM chatter and communication with the pilots of the supporting aircraft, the actual figure could be up to ten. Keen to maintain momentum and keep the enemy on the back foot, Phil informs us that the next day's patrol will be in the same area, but a little further west.

The arrival of a new chef has led to a considerable improvement in the standard of food. For breakfast, we dine *al fresco* on an area of hard standing, shielded from the sun and enemy view by camouflage netting. The food is standard ten-man ration pack fare supplemented by fresh rations; as well as bacon, eggs, baked beans and tinned tomatoes, there is sliced bread, jam and porridge, all washed down by a mug of tea or coffee. Officers and senior non-commissioned officers eat only after the men have all been fed.

After eating, I sit with some of the soldiers and listen to the banter. As someone with a vested interest in the mental as well as physical welfare of the men, I find that this proves a good barometer. I never cease to be amazed by the ease with which these impressive young men can switch from their battlefield persona of steely-eyed dealers of death to being typical nineteen-year-olds, except that as British infantrymen they will never again be typical in any way. Whilst their civilian counterparts are being ordinary teenagers, these men have set themselves apart by virtue of their training and experience. The courage under fire and selfless commitment that I have witnessed and will continue to witness over the course of this summer convinces me that I am privileged to have the best of this generation given into my care.

At around eleven in the morning, I go to bed for some welcome sleep. The camp is quiet and I assume that, with the exception of those on sentry duty or manning the operations room, most of the men are doing the same. I rise late in the afternoon for the evening routine of rehydration, kit prep, briefing and evening meal.

Geordie and Ricky take the next patrol, leaving me to stay behind and wait for the safe return of the company. I sit, fully kitted up, on the battered leather sofa in the medical facility, just in case I need to go out onto the ground. Every so often, I wander across the way and pop my head into the ops room where Dave, shirtless and chain-smoking as usual, is tracking the progress of the patrol. On my second visit, I stay for a while and listen to the radio traffic. The object of this morning's patrol is to visit Shebaz Kheyll, check whether the hamlet is inhabited and reassure the local civilians.

So far all has been quiet, but the company doesn't make it to Shebaz Kheyll. As the guys move past the southern end of Chineh, the lead platoon comes under contact. This contact consists of a series of intermittent firefights that lasts for several hours. As is so often the case, close air support is available and we give the enemy yet another hammering. The mortar line is busy once again and the camp resounds to the bass beat of salvo after salvo of high-explosive bombs being fired into enemy positions. I don't imagine that much reassurance is provided on this patrol, but the company gives the enemy another good walloping.

The contact gradually fizzles out as the Taliban realise that continuation of the attack will result in their being shredded by our superior firepower. For our part, the men have been on the ground and fighting for several hours and the longer they stay out, the lower their supplies of water and ammunition will become, making them increasingly susceptible to heat illness. As the hands on the operations room clock move round to 09.00, the company breaks contact and patrols back to base. Shortly after their return, two soldiers report to the medical facility with heat illness. One of them is only a mild case and sits in the medical facility while we supervise him rehydrating. The second man has more severe problems and needs sponging down with tepid water and a dextrose-saline IV drip.

In the afternoon one of the company jokers, a lad nicknamed Fez, brings me a 'patient'. The patient is a four-feet-long sand-coloured viper which has suffered the indignity of being decapitated. The snake was found outside our building and is delivered, still writhing, on the flat of a shovel. I'm not a fan of snakes at the best of times and, although this one is not a threat, I don't want its blood all over my doorstep. Without hesitation, I tell the soldier what he can do with the snake. Apparently, only a few days beforehand one of the guys killed a cobra that was lurking in the Afghan platoon's area of the base.

The fact that the Taliban are not the only threat in Afghanistan is underlined by a sharp knock on my door at four o'clock the next morning; I am required to treat a lad who has been stung by a scorpion. Fortunately, he is not too seriously affected. After providing him with antihistamines and pain-killers and monitoring his condition, I send the soldier back to his bed at around six o'clock.

Having been awakened early, I doze for much of the day, telephoning home in the late afternoon. I receive unwelcome news that our ageing car with its leaking head gasket has finally given up the ghost. Fortunately we have a back-up. Lisa asks me if I am in danger, to which I give a slightly cryptic response, explaining that things are interesting at times. When she asks me if I am using veiled speech, I reply that I am. I find it difficult to explain that, despite the danger, I am fine; nor can I bring myself to tell her that I am more than willing to risk my life to save that of a comrade. This has nothing to do with the politics of the war or a willingness to die for the cause; it is more a kind of *noblesse oblige* born of my profession as a nurse and my position as an officer.

After some more chat which is certainly off-limits to the reader, I wish Lisa a happy birthday for the following day and hang up the phone. I feel torn between my responsibilities as husband and father and my duty to my country. This internal conflict is not a new one, but I suspect soldiers of our generation are reminded of it more frequently than were our forefathers, who did not have global satellite phone and internet communication with their loved ones back home. I remind myself that I must concentrate on the task at hand and not allow myself to be distracted by too many thoughts of home, as that could have disastrous consequences for my patients as well as myself. I am due out on patrol at midnight to support a sniper ambush.

8 TIME SPENT IN RECONNAISSANCE

Late in the afternoon, we are told that that the intelligence picture has changed. This prompts Phil to abandon the sniper ambush. Instead 11 Platoon, supported by the CSM's party, will mount a reconnaissance patrol in the vicinity of Barikju. This small village lies on the eastern edge of the M1 wadi, more or less opposite Chineh. If the reconnaissance indicates likely enemy presence in and around the cluster of dwellings and compounds, Phil intends to use it as a potential site for a sniper ambush or standing patrol in the future.

After an evening of light sleep, I meet up with Pete. It is not a good night for a reconnaissance task: a full moon casts a silver glow bright enough for a keen-eyed observer to see us from a considerable distance. We shake out into patrol formation and leave the base shortly after 23.00. Crossing the bridge, we move out through Tangye, but instead of swinging left towards the M1 we push eastwards along a track that takes us across the eastern end of a gentle hump known as Roshan Hill. This gives us cover from any enemy dickers over in Chineh and Khovalehebad.

Our route out takes us past the Afghan national auxiliary police post. The enduring folklore of foreign armies operating in Afghanistan tells us that we can borrow an Afghan, but we will never be able to buy him. The loyalty of this assortment of tough-looking men is questionable at best and undoubtedly maintained on a *quid pro quo* basis. Indeed, there is a suspicion that the auxiliary police have passed warning to the Taliban when we have been out on patrols.

The final rendezvous point (FRV) lies about 800 metres east of Barikju, just past an isolated compound. Although there are no signs of life, somewhere in the area, possibly inside the compound, a dog begins to bark and doesn't stop. Before long, it seems as though every hound in the area has taken up the call of the wild, with at least half a dozen dogs barking and howling at the moon. So much for stealth! Soldiers love dogs, readily adopting strays and feeding them scraps of rations despite the official line that such animals are disease-carriers and should be avoided. On this occasion, I am sure that adopting this doggie is far from our minds. We move slowly past the compound, our ears and eyes straining in the gloom to pick up the sound of any movement within that might pose a threat. Nothing.

We occupy the FRV and pause to soak up the atmospherics. The dogs have fallen silent again and I can hear nothing save for the gentle wind in my ears and my own heart thumping away inside my chest. After about fifteen minutes, 11 Platoon moves off to conduct the reconnaissance task, leaving Pete, a couple of soldiers and myself to secure the FRV. We hunker down for what proves to be a long and cold wait. The blistering heat of the day has given way to a clear night that feels colder than it has done on most of our other patrols. As the wind is blowing from the north, I deduce that it could be a temporary weather front blowing down from the distant mountains that rise eastwards to eventually become the imposing Hindu Kush range.

Two hours later, those of us remaining in the FRV are beginning to have a sense-of-humour failure. We're clearly beginning to acclimatise to the heat and have not come equipped for a cold night. Donning my leather gloves and wrapping myself in a shemagh (Arabic headdress, used as a scarf) I do my best to muffle up against the cold that has stiffened my muscles and numbed my hands. As we begin our third hour of sitting still, we begin to shiver uncontrollably and make a collective decision to stand, move around and warm up, reasoning that if the Taliban were going to take us on they would have done so by now. As I stand, my half-frozen legs nearly give way underneath me; I have lost sensation in my feet and I imagine that I must look like Bambi taking his first steps. Wiggling my toes, stamping my feet and walking around forces warm blood into frigid extremities and it is not long before we pull back from the brink of hypothermia. The embarrassment of needing treatment for hypothermia in such a hot country would be too much to bear!

After about four hours, the reconnaissance has proved to be a bit of a non-event with no activity detected. Pete decides to close the FRV and relocate to a track junction south of Barikju, where we will meet up with the platoon once they have left their positions. It only takes us about ten minutes to move down to the junction, but once we are in location we have another long wait. Pete tries without success to establish communication with the platoon which, after twenty minutes, is now overdue. They are either in a radio dead-spot, or something untoward has happened.

Pete rides up the track towards their last known location, returning a short time later with a soldier hitching a ride on his trailer. As we suspected, the platoon had a communications problem. In addition to this, one of the men, the soldier on the trailer, has sprained an ankle on the rock-strewn track. I make a very quick assessment of the state of the man's ankle but defer judgement until I can do a proper examination in a warm, well-lit room. Pete gives the lad a free ride back to base while the rest of the sergeant-major's party falls in at the rear of the platoon for the walk home.

Back at Zeebrugge, I give the injured man's ankle a full check, prescribing anti-inflammatories and applying an elastic tube bandage. After giving my rifle a quick clean and taking a shower, I collapse into bed a little after 05.30.

I sleep fitfully, continually disturbed by a steady influx of soldiers reporting sick with diarrhoea. I speak to their platoon commanders and ask them to isolate the sick men from the unaffected. There is little to be done besides keeping the men hydrated and allowing the illness to take its course, which usually takes about twenty-four hours. After seeing the sick men, I am even more meticulous about hand-washing than usual as I cannot risk falling ill myself.

In the afternoon, Phil gathers the commanders in the ops room and briefs us on a patrol to Kajaki Olya which is due to take place the next day. Having focussed our efforts north of the river for a few days, it's time to switch our attention back to the south and mow the grass again.

After a short telephone call home to wish Lisa a happy birthday, I am requested by Howard, the head of the grenadier guards OMLT team, to visit his quarters. I usually drop in once every couple of days for a cup of tea and a chat, but the urgency of the request suggests that something is wrong.

The OMLT accommodation is inside the Afghan compound at the other end of Zeebrugge. I am usually wary about making my way there after dark due to concerns about the trustworthiness, not to mention the alleged sexual preferences, of some of the Afghan soldiers. When I arrive at Howard's accommodation, his colour sergeant Ty sports a grim face. There has been a supply drop that day, and it appears that the Afghan soldiers have pilfered my medical supplies. The theft was discovered when Ty was conducting an inspection of their accommodation and discovered the remnants of my medical resupply in a rubbish sack.

The Afghan platoon are told that they have disgraced themselves, and their platoon commander and his sergeant make their men stand to attention on parade for an extended period of time in an attempt at pressurising the guilty party into owning up. No such confession is forthcoming. I am shown the remnants of the medical supply; by reconciling what is present with the list of requested items, I can see what's missing. Fortunately it isn't much: a few packs of paracetamol and some antibiotics. It's hardly the crime of the century but, on principle, trust has been broken and I am livid.

To make matters worse, I find personal mail addressed to me among the medical supplies. This is a worry; if any of the Afghan soldiers are Taliban sympathisers, it doesn't take a huge leap of imagination to envisage someone contacting a relative in the UK or Europe and asking them to send threatening messages to my family at home - or worse. Howard and Ty are considering sacking the Afghan commanders.

Medical supplies are not the only new arrival today. I have been joined by a new medic, Frankie and so my medical team continues to grow! Together with Geordie, I will run some simulation scenarios to ensure that Frankie is up to speed before I commit him to operations. Until that point, he has a day or two to settle into camp routine and get some ops briefs.

I get to bed around 22.00. The rapid turnaround between day ops, night patrols and dawn patrols combined with disturbed sleep has left me utterly drained. I fall into a deep sleep but the 02.30 wake-up call comes all too soon, leaving me still tired. Once again, Kajaki Olya beckons.

It's not long before I'm back in the land of the living,

dressed and ready to go. The prep for patrol is conducted almost on autopilot. Geordie and I are on patrol today and meet up with Pete. Leaving camp by the back gate, we move on foot down to the wrecked petrol station that lies south of the ANAP guard post. There we wait for about forty-five minutes to allow the platoons to infiltrate Kajaki Olya.

We sit in the pre-dawn gloom watching for signs of enemy activity, awaiting orders to move further down the road to a new location. The order never comes; Pete has a problem with radio comms. and rides his quad bike down into town for a face-to-face discussion with Phil. About ten minutes later, the gentle purr of his bike is heard and, without dismounting, Pete tells us that we are moving back to Zeebrugge. Pete rides back to base, leaving us to follow on foot. I find myself thinking of the nursery rhyme 'The Grand Old Duke of York' and comfort myself with the knowledge that we're not the first and won't be the last soldiers to be subjected to order and counter-order.

Thirty minutes later, we arrive at the back gate and are met by Pete who updates us, letting us know that we will move out again by vehicle shortly after first light. We have time to grab a cup of tea and a bite to eat before mounting up.

The patrol turns out to be something of a non-event. We have been used to coming under contact on every patrol, but when we follow the fire support group vehicles into Kajaki Olya, it becomes apparent that we have been able to push further south than ever before. The ICOM chatter indicates that we have wrong-footed the enemy and that the Taliban fighters in Kajaki Olya have woken this morning to find themselves surrounded, resulting in stalemate. The enemy goes to ground and, despite an hour of clearing compounds, our men do not find them. Phil decides to draw the operation to a close and return to

Zeebrugge. For a change, Geordie and I have the luxury of a ride back to base. We remain fully dressed with our equipment on until we receive word that the last man in the company is safely back in camp.

Shortly after the company's return, a soldier reports sick with severe diarrhoea and vomiting. The man is badly dehydrated and unable to retain fluids. Checking him over to exclude other causes reveals nothing sinister. In addition to isolating him from his mates, I advise him to starve himself for twenty-four hours and set up an IV, giving him a litre of dextrose-saline and an anti-emetic injection.

The stolen medical supplies fail to make an appearance, so I try to call my headquarters in Camp Bastion to request a fresh supply. The satellite phone link is haphazard at the best of times; after several unsuccessful attempts, I call it quits and head to bed for a few hours of sleep.

Rising in the late afternoon, we pass the rest of the day in a relaxed manner. The electronic warfare team based up in the observation posts intercepts a communications broadcast in Pashto which suggests that the Taliban commanders are very upset about this morning's infiltration and are threatening an imminent attack on the camp. The Taliban commander is also heard stating that, should we infiltrate to that degree again, they will use suicide bombers against us. To be prepared to repel the expected attack, every man in camp stands to arms. In the days of red coats and muskets, this age-old activity would have seen us manning the ramparts. The modern take on this is more subtle. We sit, in our accommodation geared up to respond, the fire support group man their vehicles to form a quick reaction force and the guys up in the peaks are all at their posts. After about an hour of this, no attack comes and we stand down, returning to normal routine.. After reviewing the progress of the morning's patient, we pass the evening having a laptop movie night.

One of the men doesn't join us, appearing unhappy and withdrawn. When I talk to him, he tells me that he has some personal problems at home. I cannot afford to have a team member who is a liability to himself or others; however, when I offer him the opportunity to return to Camp Bastion on welfare grounds he declines, explaining that he would rather be here in Kajaki. I tell the man that I will support him in any way possible, but that I cannot tolerate having a passenger in the team. He accepts my point of view and assures me that he will not let me down. I have to take him at his word.

The next day has no planned patrol, as an operation is planned for Chineh the following day. The company spends the day in battle prep, while my growing team of medics is engaged in providing the soldiers with some additional team medic level training. The course provides infantry soldiers with some additional skills beyond that of basic first aid but, as with all new skills, maintenance of muscle memory and reinforcement of knowledge is essential to set up the men for success should they be faced with a casualty. The official ratio of team medics among the company is 1:4. By sharing the skills more widely, I hope to increase the likelihood of survival.

In the late afternoon, Phil delivers orders for the Chineh operation which will take place tomorrow. 10 Platoon will mount a standing patrol in the vicinity of Barikju, while 9 Platoon and the Afghan platoon will move out in the early hours to commence another clearance of Chineh. My medical team has grown to the extent that I can provide a luxury medical plan. For tomorrow's operation, Matt will be with 10 Platoon and I will go with 9 Platoon; V will patrol with the CSM's party under the expert guidance of Ricky. This will give V some battle inoculation and get him used to the way the company operates.

We are told that the intelligence cell has received some interesting information. In the afternoon, a group of elders from Kajaki Olya and Kajaki Sofla turned up at the Afghan national auxiliary police checkpoint and pleaded with them to ask us to push the Taliban out. The elders report that the Taliban are forcibly recruiting children into their ranks and that, if their parents do not comply, the Taliban simply kill them. Sadly, it will take more than a company of infantry to permanently clear out the bad guys, and most resources are tied up supporting the main effort further south in Sangin.

9 CHINEH AGAIN

I awake shortly after midnight, feeling as though I have been on a ten-mile run followed by a couple of rounds with Mike Tyson. Although we have had the preceding day to rest ahead of the Chineh operation, I have been busy dealing with a small outbreak of diarrhoea and vomiting among the troops. Over the course of the day I have seen seven patients, each suffering with various degrees of dehydration and nausea. The worst cases required intravenous fluids and anti-emetics; all of them have had to be isolated from the rest of the company.

This turn of events has provided me with two primary concerns: firstly, taking swift action to try to prevent the spread of the disease in order to retain as many troops as possible fit for operations; secondly, making sure that I do not succumb. I am already scrupulous about my handwashing and personal hygiene, but this outbreak makes me even more meticulous. There is nothing worse for morale and professional reputation than seeing medical personnel fall ill. The busy day has run into an evening that sees me trying to rest but caught in the grip of insomnia, made worse by my awareness of the impending patrol.

Matt has already left to cover the standing patrol mounted by 10 Platoon the previous evening, while Geordie is staying behind in camp. This leaves V, Ricky and myself to go out on the patrol as planned. I spend the last few minutes alone in my accommodation, looking at photographs of my wife and children, promising myself that I will make it home to them. My final preparation for patrol has become something of a ritual and I find that prayer grants me the ability to face up to whatever I am about to experience with courage, calmness and good humour. Prayers completed, I step outside into the darkness.

The full moon of recent days has passed and it is pitch black. As my eyes adjust to the darkness, I discern the forms of soldiers milling around and shaking out into patrol formation. I walk along the line repeating the same question.

"Nine Platoon?" I whisper.

"Not here, sir; this is the OMLT." In the darkness, I recognise the voice as being that of Ty, Howard's colour sergeant.

Moving along the line a little farther, I ask again. "Hi, lads. Looking for Nine Platoon."

"No, boss, this is Tac." This response comes from Sean, Phil's radio operator, who at thirty-seven years of age is the only man on the ground older than me and possibly the only man shorter as well.

Moving along the line, I come across two silhouettes having a quiet conversation; listening to them talk, I can tell that I'm in the right place. It's Tom, 9 Platoon's boss, and Jamie, his platoon sergeant. We shake hands and have a quick chat. I will join Jamie at the rear of the platoon and move forward with him to deal with any casualties should they arise.

Once everyone is ready, the company moves out. Because Phil is keen that the Afghan soldiers begin to present themselves as the face of our operations, the Afghan platoon will take point on the route out. This means that they will be the lead platoon and will have responsibility for the break-in to Chineh and the clearance of the first set of compounds. We move down the hill and take the now-familiar route into the northern area of operations – over the bridge through Tangye and crossing the M1 wadi at the southern end.

We are now familiar with the lie of the land and are confident that the enemy have been rolled back away from the Helmand river. In consequence, there is no need for navigation stops; listening stops are few and far between. This shortens the time taken to get to our target areas, but means that patrols are more tiring as there is practically no opportunity to take a breather. Tonight we don't stop until we reach the final rendezvous point at the base of Shrine Hill, south of Chineh. Once there, we stop only long enough for commanders to do a head count and report to Phil that their call-signs are complete.

From the final rendezvous, we follow a track that runs alongside the strip wood before gradually deepening to form a large ditch or rat run, nicknamed the Chineh bypass. This rat run passes to the east of Chineh and parallels the M1 wadi, which at this point is several hundred metres wide. Over the course of the patrol, we make our way northwards along the rat run which becomes increasingly arduous. In places the ditch has up to eight inches of fetid water in the bottom, while at various points we have to climb on our hands and knees either over or under various obstructions.

After making steady progress up the gully, we come to a halt. As I scan the M1 wadi towards the eastern horizon, I see that flickers of greyish light are pushing back the black canopy of night. Dawn is coming, as is fighting time. I have always found this time of day to be eerie. Almost everywhere I've been, I have noticed that the brief period of time between the cessation of night noises and the first birdsong of the day results in an unearthly silence. Now, before the dawn chorus, that silence is broken by the unmistakable, abrupt report of a nearby gunshot. I stiffen, anticipating that the shot will be followed by a shout of 'man down', screaming, incoming fire or possibly all three. Instead there is nothing, which in some respects is worse. Commencement of battle would constitute a near-ejaculatory release of the tension that has risen since leaving the FRV. The lack of any obvious reciprocal action serves to ratchet up the tension a notch or two further.

Notifying me that he's moving up the line to get a situation report from Tom, Jamie disappears into the gloom. I acknowledge him, settle back into a fire position and scan the area to my front and sides for enemy activity, moving my head and eyes constantly from left to right and back, moving between the foreground, mid-distance and distance. With Jamie away, there is a distance of about ten metres between me and the next man in the patrol, who is also the last man in the rear section of the platoon. Despite his relative proximity, in the half-light of dawn in Taliban land that short distance feels like a gulf, and I feel a sense of isolation at once strange and unnerving.

Jamie is gone for about fifteen minutes. When he returns, he brings some news: one of the Afghan soldiers had a negligent discharge of his rifle while moving through the first compound. No one can be sure for certain if this was an honest mistake or an attempt by a disloyal Afghan soldier to alert the enemy to our presence. As there is no way of proving it, the patrol carries on. We surmise that the Taliban must have been alerted by the shot; if they have worked out that the shot didn't come from one of their guys, there is only one natural conclusion for them to draw. Even now the enemy commanders are no doubt moving more fighters into position.

The other news that Jamie has is that we are on the move. We are going to head up the slope behind us, move past the compound that the Afghan troops have occupied and cross some open ground, before entering and clearing the next set of compounds. Clawing our way up the steep slope, we move into position and get ready for the lead section to begin the assault. While we have been making our move, dawn has broken and the new day sees us hunkered down in the lee of a small outbuilding. As the lead section moves in, we follow.

As we cross the open ground, there is a slight delay in proceedings. Jamie and I are kneeling down, waiting our turn to move, when the air is rent with the angry snap and crack of bullets passing close over our heads and the zip, zip, zip of bullets whizzing either side of us. The section which has not yet made it to the next line of buildings slides down the bank into the waist-deep ditch that the Chineh bypass has now become. I look behind me to see our interpreter heading swiftly back in the direction from which we have come, toward the safety of the building to our rear. The stream of bullets is chewing up the branches of the trees that lie to our front on the far side of the ditch. The treetops are about ten feet higher than our position, and are rapidly disintegrating into a shower of woodchips and splintering branches.

Jamie and I make a swift executive decision to follow the troops down into the ditch. It is a steep but not quite vertical drop and I move into the cover by adopting an undignified butt-slide, landing in a squelching morass of slimy mud and stinking puddle that fixes me above the ankles. Fortunately, I am able to extricate myself from the glutinous mire and move into a fire position.

When I get my bearings, Jamie has disappeared again. He has followed the balance of his platoon further up the ditch where a fierce firefight is ensuing. Whilst I am far from pinned down, there is a steady weight of small-arms fire coming in my general direction. I am thankful for the cover afforded to me by the trees and bushes that grow alongside the lip of the ditch, and even more thankful for the cover from fire provided by the ditch itself. I start making my way along the ditch to catch up with Jamie.

When I find him, he gives me a quick update on the

situation. My chief concern is to find out if there are any casualties; so far, so good. When our little conference is interrupted by some incoming small-arms fire, it suddenly becomes obvious that someone is doing their very best to kill us both. Both Jamie and I instinctively adopt fire positions and observe the area over the top of our rifle sights. About four hundred metres north, I can see green tracer fire coming our way from a small building on the other side of the M1 wadi.

As a nurse, I am armed to protect my patients under the auspices of the laws of armed conflict. Moreover, I am entitled by the inherent right to life to defend myself should anyone start shooting at me. The tracer bullets wing their way across the wadi and land about two metres in front of the edge of the ditch. Once again, the tell-tale snap of bullets above my head is worryingly close. I figure that, on this occasion, circumstances justify my returning fire. This is a big deal for me.

Although my medics wear no protective emblems (a red cross armband would constitute an aiming mark for the enemy), in the interests of self-preservation I am about to cross the line from non-combatant to participant. I have no doubt that in a court of law I would be capable of justifying each bullet fired, but it is still a daunting prospect. I zone out the sound of the bullets landing nearby, do my best to banish fear, adjust my sights and take aim at the enemy position; then I open fire.

The first three rounds of ammunition in my magazine are tracer rounds and I experience a sense of satisfaction when the first three bullets zip through the window into the enemy firing point, the fall of shot indicated by the red line that burns behind each round. I switch aim to the doorway and fire four more rounds. After each recoil action, the tip of my sight blade comes to rest on the point of aim, indicating that I am on target. No more bullets come our way. I soon realise that this is probably not my doing, as the building has attracted the fire of almost the entire company, including 10 Platoon which has now joined the battle from its position in Barikju on the eastern side of the M1 wadi.

Jamie and I move northwards up the ditch until we join up with the remainder of 9 Platoon. I feel no need to fire any more ammunition, but it is apparent that the area is teeming with enemy who are pouring fire at the company from multiple firing points to the north and east; from the far ends of Chineh and Kovalehebad and a village to the north of Barikju that we understand is named Mazdurak.

Although we do not have fast air on station immediately, we have plenty of organic firepower. The rifle platoons themselves can each pack a mean punch: each section has a 7.62-mm general purpose machine gun, a pair of 5.56-mm Minimi light machine guns and a couple of 84-mm AT4 hand-held rocket launchers. Just to add to the potential for carnage, Jamie carries a 51-mm mortar. This baby mortar has been around for decades and can fire a variety of ammunition types including smoke and high explosive. As we move along the gully Jamie pauses at intervals to fire this beast, which he manages with deft handling and impressive accuracy.

The versatility of each ten-man rifle section has been further increased by issuing the best shots with the now-obsolete L-96 sniper rifle and designating them as sharpshooters. Most of these weapon systems are used at various stages in the fight in Chineh, leaving the enemy completely suppressed and denying them any opportunity to press home any advantage they may have had at the outset. After about twenty minutes of fighting, we have air support on station. Up to six aircraft take it in turns to make attack runs against the main areas of enemy resistance to our north.

For his part, Phil is eager to keep the company balanced and break contact on his terms. After about an hour of fighting, Phil decides to conduct a controlled withdrawal and we withdraw to the final rendezvous point. This involves retracing our steps through the stinking mud of the gully. About two-thirds of the way back, Jamie comes to a halt and tells me that he will make this the platoon's rendezvous point to perform a head-count and check on his men. Jamie advises me to keep moving south to the final rendezvous point so, for the time being at least, I am on my own.

At one point, I am forced to move across a small patch of open ground at full pelt. As I break cover and sprint, a sharp-eyed enemy sees me and bursts of fire rake the ground behind me as I go. After slogging through the gully for about fifteen minutes, I emerge at the southern end of Chineh where I bump into Phil and the CSM. I am relieved to discover that there have been no casualties and that all call-signs are now beginning to withdraw. In the distance, what sounds like sporadic rifle fire can be heard. We conclude that rather than being a defiant enemy, this could be ammunition exploding in the fires caused by the bombing runs conducted by the fast jets.

The company returns to base without further event and with no casualties. After a clean-up and breakfast, notable for the excitement caused by the first fresh fruit that we've seen in a month, we have a de-briefing before getting some well-earned rest. Phil is very happy with the morning's work. I use the de-briefing as an opportunity to reinforce the message about maintaining good hygiene in light of yesterday's outbreak of diarrhoea and vomiting and today's little outing, which will have resulted in soaked boots and prolonged periods with wet feet. Good foot care is essential to the infantry soldier's ability to operate, and it is vital that commanders check their men's feet.

Later that day I receive a phone call from my headquarters in Camp Bastion notifying me that I am being joined by Matt, a doctor who will arrive tomorrow. I will have a team of four medics that I asked for and a doctor that I did not. As I contemplate how best to manage the presence of another clinician-officer, I realise that there is a reasonable chance that Matt will come bearing gifts in the form of my much-needed medical supply (to replace the stolen items) and some mail from home.

Despite having slept after the de-briefing, I have an early night and fall into a deep slumber that leaves me in a state of blissful oblivion until the following morning.

Over the next few days, Phil continues to push the company hard with a busy program of patrols, all aimed at keeping the enemy on the back foot. One evening the Taliban are detected trying to mount another attack on our base, but are foiled before they get their act together. Up in the peaks, our heavy machine guns have a clear line of fire at the enemy and estimate that they have killed a group of up to ten fighters.

Doctor Matt arrives from Camp Bastion and I take some time to orientate him and introduce him to the key players in the company. It is good to have another clinician on my team. Matt's presence causes a little confusion, as most of the men have assumed that I was a doctor myself (Captain-rank insignia plus medical equipment equals doctor). I am still sometimes asked to explain the difference between our roles and skills. The confusion is not helped by the fact that, over the last ten years, the once-clear delineation between the roles of medical officer and nursing officer have become blurred.

As I had hoped, the arrival of Doctor Matt has coincided with a resupply and mail drop. The chef receives some luxury items from Camp Bastion for his ration store including potato crisps, cookies, fresh fruit and fruit juice. When these are served as an accompaniment to our evening meal, it serves to underline how rudimentary our diet has become.

Four days after our last big fight in Chineh, we receive orders for another deliberate operation in Chineh and Khovalehebad. Phil's plan is quite complex and includes a deception plan and a feint (the distraction of an enemy by engaging him in combat). It promises to be a good fight and, despite my role as a lifesaver, I find that the war is getting under my skin and I am up for it. However, three things thwart my involvement.

First of all, JTAC Alex is ill, which means we have no means of calling in and co-ordinating close air support; secondly, it is my turn to stay in camp and coordinate the extraction and evacuation of casualties should they occur; finally and most crucially, just as the company is about to leave base for the operation, an Afghan auxiliary policeman arrives at the medical facility in the back of a pick-up truck. The policeman has been slashed across the mouth with a sharp-bladed instrument and stabbed in the chest. I am told that our patient has been attacked because he insulted another man's family, which is a big deal in this part of the world.

Fortunately, Doctor Matt has not yet left for the patrol as it takes both of us to deal with the unfortunate policeman. We check our patient for the presence of catastrophic haemorrhage before moving on to check his airway, breathing and circulation. The policeman is bleeding profusely from the facial wound, which could occlude his airway. To prevent this, we keep him sitting upright and get him to hold a field dressing to the wound. At the same time I am checking the chest; apart from a very obvious knife-sized wound on the left side, there is no indication of anything worrying. We apply a series of chest seals, but the patient is sweating so profusely that each one slides off without sticking; it is only at the fourth attempt that we succeed.

Matt gets IV access and we start running through a litre of Hartmann's solution as well as morphine and IV antibiotics. The Hartmann's is a solution of water and compound sodium lactate that is isotonic with blood and therefore an effective means of replacing lost blood volume. The best option would be to have fresh blood, but the logistic challenges push that idea into the 'too difficult' box. While I am drawing up some anti-emetic to counter the side-effects of the morphine, our man starts projectile vomiting. The vomit has a hideous brown hue, an extremely offensive odour and covers the stretcher, the treatment bay work surfaces and me. Nice! As we continue to treat our patient, I can feel some of the vomit drying in my hair while the bulk of it forms a warm, malodorous river that seeps into my combat uniform from shoulder to waist. Concentrating on the task at hand, I manage to suppress my own impulse to vomit.

Once we have our patient stabilised, I speak to Dave in the operations room to arrange a helicopter for his evacuation to the field hospital in Camp Bastion. We have a long wait; having arrived in our facility shortly after 15:30, it is 18.00 before we load our patient into a helicopter and wave him off. At around 19.00, after cleaning the medical facility and taking a shower, I discover that I've missed my allocated slot to ring home on the satellite phone. Whilst Phil lives up to his nickname and is angry that the patrol was binned, my ire is considerable when I consider that I've spent the afternoon working in squelchy, puke-covered clothing and missed my call home.

The following day, I'm out on a patrol when I begin to feel really unwell. At first I think the heat is getting to me as the daytime temperatures are now approaching one hundred and twenty degrees. However, on my return from the patrol it becomes clear that I have gone down with diarrhoea, which curtails any patrolling I might have been planning to do. Instead I take a back seat and spend the next few patrols covering the base while I recover.

One of the patrols results in a protracted and heavy firefight in which a soldier is wounded in the arm by a fragment from a rocket-propelled grenade. Geordie is about three metres away from the soldier when he is wounded and is hit in the eyes by some flying debris from the explosion; fortunately Geordie is uninjured. When the lads return from the patrol, V is particularly enthused about having seen some action. Matt and I agree to administer intravenous antibiotics to the wounded man and arrange to have him moved to Camp Bastion as a non-urgent case.

During this period, the days seem to merge into one another and become a blur of patrolling, sleeping and more patrolling. Most patrols result in contact with the enemy and we consistently get the better of them; perhaps this has something to do with our superior firepower and fast jet support.

When we're up and about between patrols, we spend our time writing letters, watching movies and talking bollocks about a broad range of subjects. One evening involves a surreal conversation about which actors we would choose to play us in a movie based on our tour. V would like to be played by Chris Rock and Geordie by one of his Newcastle United FC heroes; as a short, stocky Londoner, my choice is obvious – a young Bob Hoskins.

There is one day that stands out as memorable; my thirty-sixth birthday. As birthdays go, it is fairly unremarkable; the company is visited by General 'Jacko' Page, who doesn't have time to visit us in the medical facility. To be honest, I'm more concerned about opening the stash of birthday cards that my family has sent to me. I have also been sent some e-cards but a power outage means that I cannot reply to them, although I do manage to phone home after dinner. In the evening, we receive orders for a patrol that will take place in the early hours of the following morning to a topographic feature known as Nipple Hill, so named for its resemblance to a particular area of the human anatomy.

The purpose of the patrol is to allow the sappers to detonate some demolition charges, in order to deny the Taliban the use of a firing point there. If there are any enemy fighters in the vicinity, Phil's intent is to smash them. This will be the first time that C Company has operated in this corner of our stamping ground. Apparently the Royal Marines mounted a similar patrol there last year and lost a man in action. Rumour has it that the Taliban have a 12.7-mm Dushka machine gun in the area; if this is true, it could spoil our morning.

10 CHICKS DIG SCARS

The move out to Nipple Hill takes place shortly after midnight. It is a warm night and it does not take long for a sheen of perspiration to break out underneath my body armour. I have largely recovered from the diarrhoea of the last few days, which I now believe was due to heat illness.

I patrol with 10 Platoon, taking up my customary position at the rear with Steve, the platoon sergeant. We take the back route through the north of Tangye, crossing Roshan Hill before dropping down into the M3 wadi, which runs north east from the M1 wadi. The M3 has steep sides, lies about twenty feet deep and is wide enough to drive a light truck through.

This dry river bed consists of a combination of shingle, small rocks and boulders, making the going tough on knees and ankles. It takes about an hour of patrolling to reach the objective and when we get there, 10 Platoon moves into a position of over-watch to provide cover, while 11 Platoon conducts a clearance of a Soviet-era Russian trench system and some compounds that lie to the north.

Getting into position involves clambering over walls and roofs. As there are no ladders, we have to use the scaling techniques that all soldiers practice on obstacle courses in basic training and throughout their careers. I am glad of the repetitive 'thrashings' that we endured in our pre-deployment PT, as I have acquired the necessary strength to propel others up the walls and clamber up myself.

One of the grenadier guardsmen, a big Fijian, passes me his machine gun which I place to one side. Leaning in with my back to the wall and knees bent, I cup my hands, palms uppermost on my left knee and the guardsman places his left boot in my hands and springs off his right leg to gain momentum. As the Grenadier rises up the wall I stand, turn and extend my arms to push him upwards before passing the machine gun to him. Next, Steve gives me a leg up in the same fashion and, once I am atop the wall, the Fijian and I reach down to haul Steve up. Once on the roof, we watch and wait. We stay put for about an hour, during which time nothing happens. All goes according to plan and the engineers lay their charge. Shortly afterwards, we receive the order to begin departure.

Clambering down from the roof, we move back to the FRV point in the wadi. Once the sappers have detonated the charge, we start to make our way home for tea and medals. Having just made a bloody loud bang, the chances are that the Taliban will realise we're abroad and getting up to some mischief and they might want to come out to play. Every man is alert and on his guard.

As we patrol back down the M3 wadi, not only are Steve and I at the rear of 10 Platoon, we are at the tail end of the company snake. About ten minutes into our return journey the sound of an explosion reverberates through the wadi, bringing the company to an abrupt halt. I don't know if it is due to fatigue or general disorientation, but I feel certain that the blast comes from my rear and is a second demolition charge being detonated.

Moments later, a message buzzes in Steve's radio headset; he claps me on the shoulder and give me some unwelcome news. "Mine strike up ahead, sir," he tells me, "one times T1 casualty."

Rising to my feet, for a brief moment I have a bizarre feeling that I'm in a dream. Deep down, I knew this was going to happen sooner or later. Mines and IEDs are so prevalent in Afghanistan that we trained extensively for just this type of event before our deployment. As Steve and I head down the wadi, running past the long line of soldiers who are spread out at five-to-ten-metre intervals, Steve's platoon commander, Sam, urges caution in view of the mine threat. For my part, I have rationalised the fact that the entire company has walked this route twice this morning and has only had one mine strike. In my mind, the risk is there but it is acceptable. At this point in time, my sole purpose in life is to get to the casualty and earn my pay.

As we near the front of the company Phil stops us, urging us to proceed more cautiously. Medic Matt is already with the casualty and Sergeant Matt, 11 Platoon's sergeant, indicates a safe route in. Hurrying slowly, I remove my webbing and day-sack, place them on the ground and lay my rifle on top of them. I grab my medical kit and cautiously approach the casualty who is lying in a crater looking dazed, having suffered a very obvious traumatic amputation of his right leg.

Treading carefully and wishing that I could levitate and perform the alleged Ninja trick of retracting my testicles at will, I make my way to join Matt in the crater. As soon as I'm in, my first challenge is to convince myself that this is for real and not another training exercise - testament to the realism achieved in our pre-tour training. I start checking the wounded man, going through the C-ABC algorithm. The algorithm is designed to ensure that medics deal with life threatening injuries in descending order of priority. The first C stands for catastrophic haemorrhage. This is any massive bleed that will cause death in seconds to minutes if it is not stopped. Airway, Breathing and Circulation which are the next priorities. There is a long list of considerations to look for and treat including airway obstruction, lung injuries and less obvious bleeds, including internal haemorrhages from broken bones, abdominal and pelvic trauma. The Battlefield Advanced Trauma Life Support course that all of my team have attended has armed us with a number of useful mnemonics to guide our thinking under pressure.

Someone has already applied a tourniquet to the stump, which has stopped the bleeding. It also looks like the cauterising effect of the blast has limited the blood loss from the limb. This is a mixed blessing as the blast might well have caused blunt trauma to the man's whole body that we can do little for in the field. I move on to check the casualty's airway and breathing. As I am doing so, Medic Matt speaks up in his broad Norfolk twang to tell me that he has already done so.

"No problem," I reply. "Good job."

I move on to check for a radial pulse; it is present but rapid. This is a good sign, telling me that despite his blood loss, the wounded man is maintaining a reasonable blood pressure. Matt has given the boy some morphine, but he is still in pain. We give our patient another shot of morphine, and apply extra field dressings to the various fragmentation wounds and flash burns on his arms and legs. While Matt and I are dealing with the casualty, Phil is on the radio to headquarters to arrange the casualty evacuation. Phil tells me that the joint operations command centre in Camp Bastion is asking for a MIST report and a triage category.

The MIST report (Mechanism of injury, Injuries sustained, vital Signs, Treatment given) is a means of passing vital information about the casualty to enable the medical operations desk to make decisions about the priority for evacuation to hospital. If there is a traumatic amputation here in Kajaki, at the northern end of Helmand, and someone with a sprained ankle down south in Garmsir, it is important that the MERT helicopter is sent to the casualty with the most pressing need. I give the report aloud, which Phil's signaller then relays over the radio net. "Serial Mike: mine strike, Serial India: traumatic amputation right leg, Serial Sierra: radial pulse present, rate is 130, Serial Tango: CAT tourniquet applied, morphine given. Patient is T1."

Until now the wounded man has been passive, almost moribund, reminding me of those nature documentaries in which you see the stricken gazelle looking on with apparent calm dissociation while the lion chomps its hindquarters. However, hearing the MIST report has brought the man to his senses and the sudden realisation that he has been wounded and sustained a life-changing and life-threatening injury.

We now have a panicking casualty, which is not good; the added stress will put strain on his cardiovascular system and could cause him to hyperventilate. I do my best to calm the man down, giving him as much reassurance as I can under the circumstances. His greatest concern seems to be how his girlfriend will react to his injuries.

"You'll be all right," I tell him. "Chicks dig scars."
The nonchalant black humour doesn't have the desired effect.
"Yeah," he retorts, "they might dig scars, but they don't dig blokes with one fucking leg!"

I tell this young lad that things are really good these days and he will be fine. It sounds like a glib response, but the fact is that the standard of modern prostheses is amazing, compared with even ten years ago. My mind focuses on the present; all these concerns can be dealt with in the future. Right now, I have to deliver a live patient to the MERT team so that they can get him to a surgeon. Due to the flash burns and wounds on the soldier's arms, I can't get peripheral IV access. Instead I opt for an intra-osseous infusion, using a device to fire a needle into the man's sternum so that fluid and meds can be given via the bone marrow. Once this is done, we are under time pressure to get moving as the MERT is now airborne.

We move the wounded man on an infantry stretcher (a canvas sheet with carrying handles). Despite having six men carrying the stretcher, it is an arduous carry because the patient's weight is distributed awkwardly. If fewer than six men are carrying the stretcher, it has a tendency to sag in the middle, causing bum drag; not a good design. When we set off, 11 Platoon, to which the wounded man belongs, clears the way and 10 Platoon provides a rear guard. For most of the journey back I walk alongside the stretcher, but when some of the men are fatigued and need a change, I act as part of the bearer party. The carrying handle cuts into my hand, causing pins and needles in my fingers, while the weight of the stretcher wrenches my shoulder and sends my back muscles into spasm. My inner voice tells me to man up, as it isn't me who is going home with fewer than the usual number of legs.

When we reach the end of the M3 wadi, we cut across Roshan Hill where we meet with the CSM on his quad bike and Doctor Matt on board the Pinzgauer. We have carried the wounded man for about three kilometres. I hand the casualty over to Doctor Matt, who accompanies him to the waiting helicopter. We have earned our pay.

With the casualty offloaded, I take my place at the rear of 10 Platoon with Steve for the remaining two-kilometre trudge back to camp. I am not really focussed on the job of patrolling; instead I find myself running through the incident, second-guessing the treatment we have given and the actions that I have taken. By the time we return to base, I am confident that we could not have done more and that I would not have done things substantially differently, including running the length of the company snake in an area that is potentially mined.

After our return, we go through the customary post-patrol administration and de-briefing. Phil commends Steve and me for our courage in running to the aid of the stricken soldier before giving us a mild bollocking for failing to perform any of the drills that we're supposed to follow when there's a mines threat. I counter that we had weighed up the pros and cons in our heads and went for it anyway.

At the de-briefing, we discover that on the march out to Nipple Hill, another soldier had stepped upon a similar Soviet blast anti-personnel mine. Fortunately for him the detonator didn't work properly, producing an impotent fizz instead of a big ka-boom. Despite suffering its first amputee, C Company's luck still appears to be holding. I wonder how long this run of luck can last.

I go to bed mid-morning and snatch a few hours of sleep. In the afternoon, I stretch out in the sun-trap that is the front of the medical facility to indulge in some sunbathing. While I tan, I have a read of a good book and escape with the aid of Mahler on my personal CD player. Bliss.

In the afternoon, Phil tells me that the soldier we treated this morning has undergone five hours of surgery and will be airlifted to the UK tomorrow. We have saved his life and enabled him to make it home. Later that evening, we receive orders for a raid into the village that lies to the north of Barikju. On previous patrols, we have identified this village as the location of numerous enemy firing points. Phil suspects that it is the enemy's centre of gravity in the area. It is certainly a well-defended location and possibly the home of a command node. The village of Mazdurak, which has not hitherto featured heavily in C

Company's chat, will soon take on something of an iconic status among the men.

11 MAZDURAK

It is two o'clock in the morning. I have had a fitful sleep in the muggy atmosphere of the concrete building that I call home. Unzipping my mosquito net, I swing my legs out of bed and reach for my sandals. My bladder is full, as I drank lots of water before going to sleep.

Feeling my way through the darkened building, I find the door and waddle outside to the length of plastic guttering driven into the sand that serves as a urinal. I can smell it before I see it, the stench of ammonia carried on the warm breeze. Straining to hold in the bucketful of urine that is inside me, I move cautiously - each step threatens to make me lag my pants. After what seems like an age, I locate the urinal and briefly illuminate my target with a shielded beam of torchlight; sure of my aim, I can relieve myself. Bliss.

Many years ago, an anonymous philosopher informed me through the medium of toilet wall graffiti that the most overrated experience in life was a quick fuck, whilst the most underrated was a slow shit. If that's true, then a long and desperately-needed piss must surely come in at number two in the top ten of bodily functions. I am not sure how long I stand there but I am sure it is measured in minutes rather than seconds, rather like breaking the seal after five pints of beer on a boys' night out.

Squeezing out the last few drops, I return to my accommodation. Now that my eyes are accustomed to the dark, the return journey is easier. I tread carefully, afraid that I might step on a scorpion or snake. The curious incident of the headless snake on a shovel has stuck firmly in my mind, and I recall from my jungle training of years ago that many snakes are active at night due to the proliferation of rodents.

Back in the accommodation, I switch on the lights and give the men a kick before readying myself. Another big drink of water and some porridge oats to eat and I get dressed into proper uniform. I check my equipment and rifle, squirting oil into the working parts and working the bolt backwards and forwards. The bolt runs smoothly, the friction between the bearing surfaces eased by the oil. I listen for the tell-tale scrape that will betray the evidence of sand ingress and a dirty rifle. Nothing. Good. After a final check to listen for any rattles or clanks in my equipment, I am good to go.

As I have been prepping myself for patrol, the rest of the team have got up and are doing the same. Geordie enters the accommodation having been outside. He looks rough – pale and sweaty.

"What's up?" I ask him, thinking about the mission we have this morning.
"Got the shits, sir," he replies. "Feels like I'm ganna puke an' all."

I quickly weigh up the implications of taking an unwell man into the field and decide it is not worth the risk. I come up with a very quick and simple change of plan. Geordie will stay here as the standby medic to cover the small echelon force that maintains base security and mans the operations room. Medic Matt, until now the standby medic, will take his place and go with 11 Platoon. Doctor Matt will remain forward-based on the Pinzgauer with the CSM's group and be prepared to receive casualties from the forward platoons and work with Pete to evacuate them rearward to the helicopter landing site, where they will be retrieved by the MERT helicopter. If there is a delay in pick up, the alternative plan is to move any casualties to the medical facility. I will be with 10 Platoon.

Stepping outside into the darkness again, I walk across to the ops room. Although it is too dark to see them, I am aware of the throng of soldiers milling about. Commanders are doing last-minute checks: head counts, comms. checks, and making sure their men are prepped. Inside the ops room, I have a quick chat with Phil and Dave, letting them know about the name changes. I fill out my team's details on the flap sheet. A short time later, very quietly, C Company moves out.

Under cover of darkness, we move as quietly as possible down the metalled road that takes us down the steep hill to the front gate of the base. After crossing the bridge, we move through Tangye. Formerly the local bazaar, both sides of the main street are occupied by abandoned retail units with metal roller blinds each one identical to the last. Tangye is eerily quiet, a ghost town. As we pass each shop front, the moonlight casts our shadows onto the concrete of the buildings; a small army of silent warriors keeping pace with us on our march and mimicking our every move.

Patrolling through Tangye always reminds me of one of those scenes from a Scooby Doo cartoon, in which Scooby and the gang run along a corridor past the same four or five portraits that are repeated on a never-ending loop. It is bearable at the start of a patrol, but making the return journey in daylight at the end of a long, tiring patrol does my head in. Unlike Shaggy and the gang, the monster is not behind us, but lies ahead. In my mind's eye I can see a cartoon video of a captured man in Afghan clothes being unmasked.

"You see, all along, Terry Taliban was actually the disaffected local tribal elder who wasn't happy with losing his seat of power to the Karzai crony installed by Kabul," says Daphne. Grumbling, Mr T Taliban retorts, "And I would have gotten away with it if it hadn't been for those pesky ISAF troops!"

I remind myself to keep my sense of the absurd in check and maintain focus. "This is Afghanistan," I tell myself. "While you're daydreaming about Scooby-fucking-Doo, the local John Wayne could have you in his sight picture right now." It is a sobering thought.

Leaving Tangye behind we move cross-country, using the steep-sided wadis as cover. The mine-strike incident of two nights ago is fresh in everyone's mind and nobody wants to be a casualty. We have two options – use the wadis and be predictable, or move along the high ground and provide a choice target for anyone in the vicinity armed with an AK47, which is just about everyone in the vicinity.

We weave our way through a series of wadis which, when viewed on a map, vaguely align with a road map of Great Britain; the long, wide north-south wadi is nicknamed the M1, a large wadi running south-west from the M1 is nicknamed the M4. This morning, we are heading up the M6, vaguely paralleling the M1 wadi, bypassing a chain of abandoned villages and compounds on the eastern fringe of the M1. I have tried my best to memorise the place names on the big map in the operations room. In addition to our favourite haunts of Chineh, Kovalehebad and Barikju, there are other places that we have not yet visited - Akwan Kheyll, Bagar Kheyll, Shomal-i-Gulbar, Mazdurak.

Many locations are not named on the maps, but have been given names by various units as their locations carry operational significance. These include: Blue Pipe compound (a compound with blue hosepipe running through it), The Shire (a group of buildings named for their resemblance to the hobbits' houses in the *Lord of the Rings* movies), Ant Hill (a hill that resembles a large ant hill) - you get the picture.

The march from COP Zeebrugge to Mazdurak takes about an hour. Each man is carrying about 80 lbs of equipment and ammunition; the troops are heavy on ammunition and water, light on luxuries. I carry a packet of dried fruit army biscuits in my pocket, the rest of my burden is ammunition, water and medical equipment. As well as the medical pack that I carry on my back, every available pocket I have is stuffed with spare field dressings, tourniquets, latex gloves and chest seals: all the stuff that will save a man's life if he is in danger of bleeding out from a catastrophic haemorrhage.

Although we are working at night to beat the heat, the weight of kit we are carrying leaves us drenched in perspiration from the exertion. Leaving the M6 wadi, we move up a rat run (a deep, narrow ditch) that runs northward and brings us up level with the east side of Mazdurak. The men close up and take up firing positions, observing their arcs of fire for signs of enemy movement; the word goes down the line that we are at the line of departure for the clearance of Mazdurak.

Mazdurak: we have not been this far north before. The purpose of this raid is to conduct a bit of a reconnaissance in force, find out about the enemy strengths and dispositions, stir up a fight and then break off and head for home. Judging by the amount of incoming fire we have had from Mazdurak on previous patrols, I anticipate that it is going to be a bit like poking a great big stick into a large hornets' nest.

Checking my watch, I see that it is 04.45. The murky darkness is beginning to dissipate as the first glimmers of daylight appear on the horizon. Tommo, one of the section of Grenadier guards attached to 10 Platoon, holds up his hand to show all five digits; this indicates that we will move in five minutes. Everything that we have learned about this area so far tells us that the enemy are close by. It gives me a good feeling to know that over one hundred soldiers have penetrated deeply into enemy territory under the cover of darkness.

This is the beginning of the break-in designed to gain a foothold in Mazdurak. 11 Platoon leads, running in single file across a 200-metre stretch of open ground before reaching the first compound; they are in without a shot being fired. 10 platoon is next, following the same route in; moving through 11 Platoon's position in the first compound to launch onto the next. Tommo is the last man in the third section; then it is me, followed by Steve, the platoon sergeant. As I get up and start running, half of me is convinced that I will be dead before I reach the safety of the compound and the other half is saying, "Game on!"

I run as hard and fast as I can to get across the open ground as quickly as possible. The route I take is a well-worn track bordered by swathes of opium poppies that grow chest-high. Each step carries me closer to the safety of the compound, but means a moment longer of potential exposure to enemy fire.

Over the course of that joyful little sprint, I have the opportunity to consider what might happen should I be hit. The answer opens up a series of 50:50 possibilities: I will live or die. If I die, I will experience an afterlife or eternal nothingness. If I experience an afterlife, it will be heaven or hell. If I am hit and killed, my best hope is that it will be over in an instant with no pain. If I am hit and survive, a whole load of worrying possibilities arise: immense pain, disability and disfigurement. Whether I live or die, either way a whole lot of shit would be heading towards my wife and family. Processing all of these variables takes only a few seconds, and I do the only thing that will guarantee my sanity - I take these worries and bury them deep into my subconscious to deal with on another day.

I enter the compound at a point where the high wall has been reduced to a low pile of rubble. Scrambling over and making my way in, I see that the compound is actually a large walled garden about the size of a football field, maybe a little bigger, cultivated with flowers and fruit trees with an open well in the centre. Under different circumstances, it might be a pleasant place to sit and while away the morning - under different circumstances.

11 Platoon has occupied the far end of the garden and is in position, ready to cover the launch of 10 Platoon onto the next compound. Behind me, Phil's Tac HQ party has joined us. I can overhear a garbled and tinny radio conversation coming from the handset that Phil's radio operator has clipped to the yoke of his webbing. The conversation is clear enough for me to recognise the disembodied voice of Mark, the fire support group commander, who has positioned his vehicles on a ridgeline overlooking Mazdurak.

Phil is living up to his 'angry' nickname, giving orders to speed 10 Platoon's move into the next compound. I like Phil and feel that, in the few weeks we have worked together, we have created a bond of mutual trust and professional respect. He strikes me as having the right mix of ruthlessness, compassion and empathy that make for a good field commander.

The Vikings have a family ethos that binds them together and, not for the first time, these soldiers strike me as the best of their generation, proving their ability to match the reputation of their forefathers. All the officers in C Company command the respect of their men. 'Classless' is the word that the battalion uses to describe itself; this is certainly accurate, but by the day's end I will decide upon another adjective to describe them: peerless.

10 Platoon's assault onto the next compound involves another dash of death across open ground. Not as far this time, but perhaps more dangerous as it is now almost broad daylight. There are plenty of positions, nearby and in depth, from which the enemy might observe us, open fire or call his own indirect fire support onto us. Fortunately, the entire platoon makes it into this compound without event.

Our new compound looks as if it were once a house of impressive proportions. Apart from the outer wall, it has mainly been bombed to shit. A couple of side rooms are intact, but for the most part it is a rubble-strewn mess through which we have to pick our way with care to avoid ankle sprains. I settle myself down in a corner while one of the sections lines up in single file next to a doorway through which it will burst to clear the rest of the compound. I look at my watch; it is 05.10 and unnaturally quiet, as though the very fabric of the village knows what is about to happen and is holding its breath.

The section which is about to start clearing the rest of the compound makes its move. Breaking down into two-man assault teams, they start the process of leap-frogging from room to room with fixed bayonets. A second section moves through after them, along with Sam, the platoon commander.

A short time later - I'm not sure if it's seconds or minutes, as my perception of time is affected by the tension - the unmistakable staccato rattle of a burst of AK47 fire pierces the silence. Merging with the din of automatic fire is the sound of two or three single shots in angry retort. For a split second all is quiet, as though everyone, British and Taliban, is working out what to do next. I don't have to wait long until the urgent shout of "Man down!" echoes through the compound.

I'm on my feet and moving. As I do so, the world around the compound erupts into battle. I can see nothing beyond the thick mud walls, but the volume and rate of small-arms fire and the muffled grenade explosions makes it clear that somewhere off to my left the bulk of 10 Platoon is engaged in a heavy firefight, while 11 Platoon and Tac are also under contact in the walled garden. Making my way to the top end of the compound, I find Steve, who is on the radio getting an update about the casualty.

"What's the score?" I ask anxiously. The clock started ticking for this casualty the moment he was hit. My inner voice taunts me with the reason for my presence on the battlefield: "Give the surgeon a live patient. Give the surgeon a live patient." Steve fixes me with a look of concern. "Gunshot wound to abdomen," he tells me, "T1", meaning the highest triage priority for treatment.

My inner voice goes into panic mode. "Fuuuuck!" I steel myself for what I am about to receive (may the Lord make me truly grateful). I imagine a horrendous gaping wound with viscera and intestines hanging out, blood and shit everywhere. This," I tell myself, "is where you earn your pay."

Steve tells me that the men are evacuating the casualty to our location, so all I have to do is stay put and wait. In the meantime, he has a battle to run. Tommo and his section of Grenadier guardsmen – the G-men - have moved up and are poised to go through the double gate in front of us and assault the next compound to our north. The G-men are revved up and I offer them some words of encouragement as they move off to an accompanying chorus of 51-mm mortar bombs, courtesy of Steve.

Just as the G-men are launching their assault, the wooden door behind me is flung open. A group of men burst into the compound, led by Bomber, one of 10 Platoon's section commanders. Bomber is calling for my assistance; two of the men are half-carrying, half-dragging the casualty between them. Together we move the wounded man and sit him down, propped against a wall. I reach into my pocket, grab a field dressing, put on a pair of latex gloves and kneel down to examine him.

There are no signs of a catastrophic haemorrhage, and the man's is breathing spontaneously with no obstruction or injury to his airway. The wounded man is C, Sam's radio operator. I ask him to count from one to ten in a single breath, which he does. C's capacity to do this tell me that there is no respiratory compromise at present and also indicates that sufficient oxygen is reaching the brain to enable him to obey commands – two important items of information. There is also a two-fold fringe benefit to C doing this: not only does he have something other than his injuries to focus on, but also it is such an unusual thing to be asked to do that he is probably wondering why the hell I have asked him to do it, instead of worrying that he might be about to die.

While I am conducting my tactical rapid primary survey, a significant firefight has erupted nearby. Steve and Bomber have been engaging the enemy next door with a combination of rifle fire, 51-mm mortar bombs and light machine-gun fire. I decide that the best thing for me to do is to zone out the noise of battle and focus on the wounded man. If I can convince C that treating men with abdominal gunshot wounds in the middle of a firefight is an everyday occurrence for me, I'll be happy.

I open C's body armour and cut back his shirt to expose the chest. Both sides of the chest are rising and falling evenly and there are no apparent signs of blunt or penetrating chest trauma. So far, so good. A bullet has grazed his trapezius muscle, but is not life-threatening.

I quickly check the man's radial pulse; it is present and bounding along at about one hundred beats per minute, both good indications that there is currently no massive haemorrhage. Having run through the key potential checks that would indicate an imminent threat to life, I focus on the obvious and start to check his abdomen; front, sides and back. There is an obvious entry wound at the lateral aspect of the right lower quadrant and a corresponding exit wound on the bottom-right side of his back. No shit, no guts, just a moderate amount of haemorrhage. I almost start laughing. "You're one lucky bastard," I tell him. "It has missed everything important!"

It is miraculous. The bullet, having entered his abdomen at an oblique angle below the lower edge of his body armour, has tracked through fatty tissue and his external oblique abdominal muscle and exited stage left without hitting anything. I dress his wounds with field dressings and inject a shot of morphine into his leg. With help from one of the soldiers, I strip him of his kit and make sure that his ammunition is redistributed.

During the course of my consultation, Tommo's G-men have fallen back to our compound, overwhelmed by the weight of enemy fire; they have been beaten back. I'm not yet aware of the fact that one man is missing from their number; guardsman A, a likeable young lad to whom I've spoken a few times, has been hit. His comrades haven't managed to get to him, but thankfully he has had the presence of mind to crawl and then run back to our compound. I learn later that, despite his injuries, A has drawn a sketch map in the dirt to indicate the exact position of the enemy.

The first awareness I have that A has been hit is when I see him. I have just finished dressing the first man's wounds when A comes staggering towards me. He has a head wound and is bleeding from the nose, looking dazed. He has his morphine autoject in his hand, but thankfully hasn't used it; morphine could make him drowsy and mask signs of serious complications caused by his head injury..

Sitting A down, I check him over, conducting the standard tactical rapid survey. The only injury is a gunshot wound to his temple which has fractured his orbit. His right eye is closed by swelling so marked that his temple bulges out to the side. I dress his wounds and get one of the guys to keep talking to him, to make sure that he doesn't drift into unconsciousness. C is stable and likely to remain so, but A is a different matter; when the bullet hit his temple, it would have been travelling at around 700 metres per second. With high velocity gunshots, it is not the bullet itself that does the most damage, but the shockwave of kinetic energy that follows behind it. When this force meets a solid object, the kinetic energy is transferred into it, causing damage to bone and tissues over an area that far exceeds the diameter of the bullet. It is likely to have caused all sorts of underlying tissue damage to A's brain. I need to get him out of here fast!

Air cover comes on station in the form of fast jets and Apache helicopters. The Taliban are getting a real thumping and we are able to break contact. Once we have fallen back close to our entry point into the compound, Steve organises the evacuation of the two casualties. I try to persuade C that he needs to be carried on a stretcher but he respectfully tells me to fuck off. Remembering to address me as 'sir'; he points out that he is rather large and that the others will struggle to carry him. I acquiesce and help him to his feet; he manages to walk by himself. Steve lifts A and hoists him into a fireman's lift; followed by C, who moves as fast as he can manage, they run the gauntlet of enemy fire back to the walled garden, where they will be looked after by Medic Matt until they can be evacuated by Pete and his magic quad bike.

I am left on the position with Tommo's section and some of Bomber's. As the only officer present, I go in among the men and ensure that we are prepared to mount a hasty defence in the event of a Taliban counterattack. I grab hold of M, the big Fijian machine-gunner, position him at a vulnerable point and provide him with arcs of fire. One of the G-men, A's best mate, is weeping. He is only a young lad and is understandably shaken up. I employ him to help me sort out my medical kit to keep him busy and try to occupy his mind.

In the meantime Sam has arrived with the remainder of the platoon. After running another dash of death, Steve rejoins us. We pull back into the walled garden. Phil has given orders that we are to break contact and withdraw to the FRV, from which point we will start back to COP Zeebrugge. After a quick headcount, we move as planned.

Back in the walled garden, there has clearly been something of a fight. The compound is wreathed in smoke and the acrid tang of cordite itches in the back of my throat. There is lots of toing and froing as company gets ready to withdraw. The casualties are already being transported back to Doctor Matt's location in the M6 wadi, where he will check them over and stabilise them for onward evacuation by helicopter. We are well shielded by the compound walls so, despite the enemy still firing at us, we are relatively safe. A sudden flash of flickering bright light fills the compound, followed by an explosion. For a moment, I am dazed and don't register what's going on. Although my ears are ringing, I can hear someone shouting for a medic.

Looking across the compound, I see a man face down and sprint to where he is lying. The man's arms lie limp by his sides and my first impression is that he is dead. When I roll him onto his back to check, his body is flaccid and difficult to move but the movement brings a low, animal-like groan. I have heard this sound before, many years ago when I nursed a man with severe head injuries. There is no massive haemorrhage visible, so I check his airway. The casualty's breathing is shallow and rapid; a quick check of his radial pulse tells me that he is maintaining his blood pressure for the moment. Fearing more incoming fire, I enlist the help of the wounded man's mate to move him somewhere a little less exposed, close to one of the compound walls. As I begin to check my patient, I hear someone else calling for assistance.

Not having realised that there's more than one casualty, I look up and see that Manie, 11 Platoon's commander, is kneeling alongside another body. This scene unfolds before my eyes but the realisation only sinks in after five seconds or so. For a moment I am overcome with disbelief. "That's four casualties this morning," I tell myself. "Will there be more?"

My inner voice is not my best friend today and raises the issue of how to balance my sense of duty with the self-preservation instinct. "What if you're next?" taunts the voice. I have tried to suppress this question since that first dash of death into this very compound about an hour ago. Once again I forcefully quash the thought and don't allow it to resurface.

Moving the first man seems to have jolted him back from

the brink of unconsciousness, but he's not in good shape. His eyes are open, but there is a vacant look in them which unsettles me and he is clearly having difficulty breathing. I ask his mates to start dressing some of his wounds, telling them that I will be back. Running across to where Manie is kneeling, I check on the other casualty.

The second man was caught in the same explosion as the first, but managed to walk away before collapsing. I don't need to look hard to find a catastrophic haemorrhage; a blood-red swamp is expanding rapidly across the fabric of his combat trousers, soaking him from waist to knee. Frantically ripping away his body armour, I grab my scissors and cut away his uniform. A football-sized balloon of blood is forming in his abdomen above the pubic bone. Deep in his groin is an entry wound so small that I can't get a finger into it. We've been issued a special haemostatic dressing for this kind of wound, but the wound is too small even for the dressing.

If this were a Hollywood movie I would be able to get some forceps up into the wound and clamp off the artery, but in reality it would be like searching for a needle in a haystack. Desperately, I rip open a field dressing and get Manie to apply pressure to the groin wound with it. Judging by the size of the swelling and the pool of blood seeping into the sand, I estimate that the soldier, N, has lost at least two litres of blood. The only extra move I can think of is to apply direct pressure to the swelling above N's pubic bone. I press down hard with both hands, applying all the force I can muster. N does not like this, but I tell him I need to stop the bleeding.

After applying pressure for a few minutes, I secure the field dressing to his groin, wrapping it as tightly as possible. Miraculously, N has remained conscious and capable of speech throughout this process. A quick check of his chest and back reveals no injury and I am pleasantly amazed that he still has a palpable radial pulse in spite of his blood loss. I grab some casualty straps from my medical kit and bind them tightly around his pelvic girdle and thighs to reduce the likelihood of any clots being dislodged and starting the bleeding again.

Taking no chances, I borrow a sling from a general purpose machine gun and use that to secure his feet and ankles with a figure of eight. I am about to give N a shot of morphine until he tells me that he doesn't want it. I am impressed by his toughness, but offer it again; I don't like to see people in pain and these wounds must hurt. Again, he refuses any analgesic. We move N across the compound and position him next to the other casualty so that I can continue to work on them both.

Switching my attention to the first man, S, I resume the assessment that had been curtailed by the urgent need to treat N. There is no catastrophic bleed and S is maintaining his airway, but his breathing is rapid and shallow. Exposing his chest reveals a mass of fragment wounds across both sides. I instinctively reach for a chest seal, but find that the adhesive backing will not stick to his chest. I try three times and use extra tape, but to no avail. If I cannot get a seal, the Heimlich valve will not perform its job of removing air from the pleural membranes and allowing the lungs to re-expand. I ditch the chest seals in temper, angry that we have an item of kit that doesn't seem to do the job for which it is designed.

While I am doing this, the Taliban are pressing home an attempt at a counterattack and our machine-gunners are firing over the top of the compound wall. We have a pair of USAF A-10 Warthogs on station and these airborne leviathans take turns to make strafing runs on a group of enemy presumably close to the other side of the wall. The cannonade sounds as if it's within tens of metres of me and my open-air emergency room.

The strafing sounds like the sort of noise one might expect to hear if Satan was moving his furniture around. Imagine the sound of a dump truck shedding a load of large ball-bearings from a great height, multiply it by a hundred, and you might have some idea of the sound of the cannons firing. Immediately after that, the air is filled with the high-pitched scream of the aircraft pulling out of its dive and returning to height. Although the noise of a pack of hell-hounds would probably be more soothing, the sound is music to my ears as it means that the pilot is covering our backs.

A short distance away, three men are standing over an overheated machine gun, urinating over the barrel to cool it. Drinking water would be too precious to use for this and there is a readily available supply of the alternative fluid. The rank stench of vaporised piss permeates the air and almost makes me gag. The gunner wipes some stray drops of urine off the carrying handle with the cuff of his shirtsleeve before picking the gun up to place a fresh belt of ammunition into the feed tray.

I realise that S needs placement of a chest tube or a needle decompression to improve his breathing, but with the fighting going on around me and fast jets screaming in to break up the counterattack, I don't trust myself to perform either procedure safely and tell myself that this is neither the time nor place. For now at least, 'scoop and run' will be better than 'stay and play'. I make it known that we urgently need to move both casualties off the ground. We are fortunate that Geordie, temporarily off his sick-bed, has moved to the landing site near the base to coordinate the load of the first two wounded men. On hearing from Dave in the ops room that there are more casualties,

Geordie has taken the initiative and persuaded the helicopter to stay put while we evacuate them.

10 Platoon provides the manpower to evacuate the casualties - six men on each stretcher and a team to provide flank protection. With covering fire from Mark and the fire support group, we move back to the rat run with the angry whizzes and cracks of bullets, both friendly and enemy, passing over us and in between us. It is a miracle that nobody else is hit.

Just behind the rat run, Pete is waiting with his quad bike and trailer. N and S are transferred onto proper stretchers and strapped down onto the trailer. I scribble some quick handover notes and hand them to the CSM to give to Doctor Matt. Something that has been bugging me is the whereabouts of Medic Matt, who should have been with 11 Platoon. I ask the sergeant-major, who tells me that Matt has been hit. When they were loading the first two casualties onto the quad bike, a mortar bomb exploded nearby. Pete, 11 Platoon's sergeant (another Matt) and Medic Matt were blown off their feet. All are okay except for Medic Matt who has been wounded in the leg by fragments of the mortar bomb casing and will be flown out with the other casualties.

The sergeant-major revs the quad bike and heads off back to the rendezvous with the helicopter. Once the company is complete in the rat run, the platoon sergeants account for their men and Phil gives the order to withdraw. Fire from the heavy machine guns up on the peaks cover our movements and we run in single file, one bound at a time, back to the M6 wadi.

At the junction with this wadi, 10 Platoon provides all-round defence to cover the extraction of 11 Platoon and Phil's Tac HQ. For the first time since initiating contact with the enemy, I have a moment to think about what has just happened. Tommo is walking down the line dishing out cigarettes to his men. "Want a smoke, sir?" he ask, offering me a battered-looking packet of cigarettes. "No, thanks, I don't smoke," I reply. Tommo grins. He shakes his head, pulls a cigarette from the packet and offers it to me again. "No, sir, have one; you fucking need it!"

Dumbfounded, I put the cigarette between my lips and light it, inhaling deeply. It's at least four years since my last cigarette. Momentarily overwhelmed by this simple act of kindness and the tension of the morning's work, I begin to sob quietly, apologising at the same time. I feel ashamed at showing such weakness in front of the men but can't help myself. Tommo pats me on the shoulder and moves on down the line, dishing out more smokes.

Snapping out of my moment of self-pity, I get a grip on myself and start moving up the line in the opposite direction to Tommo to check on the men. "Any injuries, lads? Any problems?" I ask. One of the guys, M, tells me that he has a grenade fragment in his leg. I offer to look at it but he declines, telling me he'll come to see me later. I carry on smoking the cigarette, inhaling deeply. It burns my lungs and makes me cough, but I find the action of placing hand to mouth and inhaling quite therapeutic. Warning myself that I mustn't make it a habit, I feel guilty for having smoked at all; my wife is a former Great Britain athlete and my stepdaughters are budding swimmers, all of them vehement anti-smokers. They wouldn't understand why I found a cigarette so soothing to my jarred nerves this morning. Thinking of home, I wonder what will happen to my family if I am killed or wounded here. It seems quite impossible to explain to my wife and family what has happened this morning.

It has been a tough morning. Once 11 Platoon and Tac

join us, we shake out into staggered file formation and patrol back to camp, retracing our route back through Tangye. The sun is rising higher in the sky and the heat of the day is upon us. On the way back to camp, I conduct a post mortem of my actions. The images of the wounded men seem to flash through my mind's eye in an endless, grotesque slideshow. Eventually we find ourselves crossing the bridge and making the energy-sapping ascent back up the steep hill to COP Zeebrugge. As I climb, the WMIK Land Rovers of the FSG come whizzing past.

Trudging the last hundred metres up the hill to my accommodation saps my strength. The adrenalin rush that has kept me in overdrive for much of the morning has receded, leaving me dog-tired, nauseous and hungry. I am reminded of Ernie Pyle's classic piece of reportage from World War II in which he likens the march of exhausted US soldiers to that of automatons, rocking almost mechanically from side to side with each pace; tired, relentless, unceasing. I flatter myself with the thought that this is how I might appear to an onlooker.

Arriving at the medical facility, I am greeted by Geordie and Doctor Matt; we exchange a few pleasantries as I unload my rifle and strip it down for cleaning. As we chat, we piece together the events of the morning. When I ask about Medic Matt, they tell me that he took a lump of mortar fragment in his knee; he had not seemed too bad when he was helped aboard the helicopter, but there might be more extensive damage. Apparently, on arriving at the rendezvous, he reported to Doctor Matt that he had given himself morphine but had been unable to write the letter M on his cheek, as he couldn't see what he was doing. In the absence of medical notes, it is standard practice to write the letter M and the time of administration on casualties' cheeks to indicate that they have received morphine, thereby reducing the likelihood of an accidental overdose. This makes us all fall about laughing, mainly because of Doctor Matt's impersonation of Medic Matt which is spot-on. Although we are a little cruel to have a laugh at Matt's expense, it is just banter and the humour is tempered by a genuine concern for a friend. The reality that one of my team has been wounded in action will not hit home until Geordie and I box his kit up the following evening.

Task Force Helmand has initiated Operation Minimise, which is standard practice whenever troops have been wounded or killed. All personal and non-official communications are banned until the next-of-kin of the casualties have been notified. The idea is to ensure that families are told officially by a casualty notifying officer, and not through Facebook or a well-meaning but misinformed telephone call or email.

I have just finished cleaning my rifle when it is time to attend the de-briefing in the operations room. We sit on the chairs and benches facing the big ops map; each of the platoon commanders and platoon sergeants is present, along with representatives from the supporting arms and services. The events of the morning are subjected to a thorough post-mortem; any critical points, good or bad, are teased out and consideration is given to how things might run better in future. Phil provides us with an update on the casualties and confirms that all have survived the journey to Camp Bastion. A and S are both listed as seriously ill. All of them will be evacuated to the UK and none will be back in the line any time soon.

Once the de-briefing is over, I just have time for a shower before breakfast is served. It is 10.00 by the time I collapse into my bed for a sleep which, despite tiredness, does not come easily. Whenever I close my eyes I see A's bloodied and broken face. Doctor Matt has confided in me that, of all the casualties, he thinks A and S might not survive. Eventually I fall into a deep sleep, so deep that when I wake up I'm not sure who I am, let alone where. I've asked Matt to wake me no later than 15.00 as I have a briefing at 16.00 for the next patrol.

The next patrol is supposed to be a big affair into Kajaki Olya again, just to let the enemy in the south know that we haven't forgotten about them. However, the patrol is cancelled when we receive two pieces of intelligence. The first is that the enemy have apparently mined the area that we were due to focus on. The second is that a large number of Pakistani fighters have moved in to Kajaki Sofla (south of Kajaki Olya) with the intention of trying to overrun our modest outpost. Instead of concentrating on the south again, Phil switches his attention to the north; the day after the cancelled operation we are on our way back to Nipple Hill, this time in daylight.

12 STAY SAFE BROTHERS

On the day after our fight in Mazdurak, the hot news is the battle damage assessment that comes from a local intelligence source. The estimate is that C Company killed twenty-two Taliban fighters and wounded thirteen more. Phil is keener than ever to maintain the pressure on the enemy and keep the company busy, hence another big patrol is mounted today. It is my turn to stay behind while Ricky, Geordie, V and the doc go out on patrol. There is lots of ICOM chatter, but no actual contact; as always, it is a relief to see the company return safely, particularly after the events of the last few days.

The campfire chat among the troops at mealtimes is more subdued than usual and it seems as though the reality of the tour has hit home. One young soldier, who looks barely old enough to serve, confidentially tells me that he would happily go home now. His view is that he has proved himself in combat, but is in no hurry to see any more friends wounded or become a casualty himself. If there are many more days like Mazdurak, he might not be alone. While I can empathise with him, young as he is, this man volunteered and signed up for this. Back in the days of the pre-9/11 army it could have been argued that he had been enticed into the ranks by the lure of learning a trade or gaining life-skills with the army downplaying the reality of life in the infantry in a shooting war. Since 2001, footage of the campaigns in Iraq and Afghanistan and news coverage of soldiers' deaths have been regular features on TV and cyberspace and have hardly been downplayed. For me, the once-plausible case for misrepresentation of the facts of army life no longer holds up.

Following Mazdurak, I have experienced something of a reality check of my own. Whereas only a few days before I was quite disgruntled at the plan to move me back to Bastion after another week or two, I am starting to think that, if there are many more patrols like the raid on Mazdurak, I will just be glad to make it out of here in one piece.

Another hangover from the fight in Mazdurak is the handful of men who report sick over the next couple of days. One man comes in suffering from tinnitus, resulting from prolonged noise exposure. Another guy, the big Fijian guardsman, comes to see me to sort out grenade fragments that remain in his arm and knee. This man is singularly impressive; not only did he carry back from Mazdurak his own machine gun and equipment, but also the kit and weapons of the wounded. I now know that he did this with injuries of his own.

I discuss his case in a telephone conversation with the senior medical officer in Camp Bastion, who strongly recommends that the man comes in for an X-ray and surgical opinion. When I give this news to the Fijian soldier, he pleads with me to not be sent back in, explaining that this would be seen as dishonourable in his culture. I am moved beyond words by the selflessness and soldierly virtues of this man. The best I can do is strongly recommend that he goes in for his own welfare, but explain that I cannot force him against his will. In the end, this legend of a man acquiesces and goes back to Camp Bastion; he returns within a couple of days.

The clinical conference call is not the only communication that I have with Camp Bastion. I receive a telephone call from our regimental second-in-command, who congratulates us on our work in dealing with the casualties of the last few days. It's a pleasure to pass on the message to my team at our evening briefing. As a result of our actions there are six men who are on their way home to their families with a good chance of recovery; it is a good feeling and gives me a real buzz.

It is three o'clock in the morning and I can't sleep. The patrols of the last few days have been taxing, and Mazdurak is on my mind. When we went into Mazdurak, over the course of a two-hour battle the company suffered five men wounded, four of them severely. Then there's M, the mine strike victim; of all the casualties, his wounding seems to have had the most impact on the young lads in C Company. From talking to the men, I gather that the fear stems from two distinct issues: the nature of the weapons and the injuries they inflict.

As a soldier, you convince yourself that to some extent your destiny is influenced by your fitness, skilled handling of weapons, marksmanship, field-craft and a degree of good fortune. This is largely true in a straightforward firefight; however, with anti-personnel mines your chances of survival are largely down to luck. Unless you detect the ground sign of a dug-in mine (unlikely in the dark), you are just as likely to become a victim as the next hapless man. Likewise, if you get hit by a bullet, you know one of two things will happen: you will either live or die. If you are wounded your injuries might only be light, such as a bullet graze. The man targeting you might even miss. The thing about mines is that they don't generally miss, and you can't levitate over them in the same way that you might choose your route across the ground to avoid rifle fire. When you step on that mine (and you won't know it's there until you do), there is only one outcome – being blown off your feet and possibly leaving one or both of them behind.

The point I am making is this – although you arrive on tour knowing that men can and do become wounded and killed, in your mind it is always something that happens to someone else. As time goes on, you witness the chaos of combat and the effect of hot flying metal on human flesh, and come to the realisation that it could happen to you too and there is very little you can do about it.

Along with Medic Matt, I dealt with M when he lost his leg. The following day, I dealt with most of the casualties in Mazdurak; the only one I didn't see was Medic Matt himself when he was hit by shrapnel from a mortar bomb. Six weeks into the tour, I have reached the point at which I realise that I am not bullet-proof and this has had a profound effect on me.

I am not too bad when actually out on patrol; I usually have too much to think about to be concerned about my own safety, particularly if there are casualties to treat. When I am back in from patrol, the routine of life in the base keeps me focussed and busy; holding sick parades, attending briefings and conducting medical training for the platoons. The worst time for me is at night, when the erratic sleep pattern brought about by irregular patrolling leaves me wakeful and preoccupied. Then I have time to think and the opportunity to consider the consequences for myself and my family should I be wounded.

In some respects, medical insight makes the worry worse. Whilst I can take solace from knowing that my chances of survival exceed those of soldiers from any conflict in military history, I also have insight into what survival might entail. My mental list reads like a 'Who's Who' of bad clinical outcomes: paralysis, coma, diminished cognitive or motor function, urinary catheterisation, colostomy, incontinence, erectile dysfunction, traumatic castration, double or triple amputation, hemianopia, dysphasia, epilepsy and much more.

Weighing all of this up in the early hours of the morning, I cannot decide whether or not I would prefer death to severe maiming. If I were maimed at least I would see my family again, but how would my wife react? Would she find the prospect of becoming a carer for a broken-bodied soldier too much to bear and leave me? If that were the case, I think I might prefer to be dead.

I look at my watch, it is four o'clock. An hour has passed while I have been contemplating the worst outcomes that military life could throw at me. For some reason, I think of the scene at the beginning of the classic movie *A Bridge Too Far*. A sergeant named Eddie, played by a young James Caan, is giving his captain a pep talk ahead of the jump into Arnhem. The captain is convinced that he's going to be killed in action and seeks a guarantee from the enlisted man that he won't die. The captain is drinking strong alcohol which the sergeant pours away, telling him that drinking won't help him. When the captain asks what will, Eddie's response is simple – not getting shot.

Not getting shot, not stepping on a mine, not being the poor bastard in the wrong place when a brief high-pitched shriek announces the imminent impact of a 107-mm rocket: all of that will help. How to manage it? You tell me!

After a while I drift off back to sleep and doze fitfully. I am due out on a patrol at 07.00. We're leaving it a little later today to let the enemy think we're not coming out to play, hoping that they won't be expecting us. When it's time to get up, it doesn't take long to sort out my equipment; my kit was packed anyway and my rifle is clean. All I need to do is to shower and dress and have a bite to eat.

Ten minutes before we form up to move out, I thumb through the photocopied leaflet of prayers for the soldier which has been kindly provided by the Royal Army chaplains department. I gaze at the pictures of my wife and children, running a finger over the images of their faces, and wonder if I will ever see them again. Tears prick at the corners of my eyes and I allow myself a solitary sob. Geordie knocks on my door without entering; he too is geared up for patrol. "Five minutes, sir!" he announces. It resembles a cue-call to an actor for their big moment on stage. "Cheers, Geordie. I'll be there in two," I reply.

Folding up the photos, I replace them in the small cardboard box that contains my letters and personal effects. I gather up the crystal stones that I carry in the hope that they will keep me grounded, calm and courageous and tuck them away in the small pocket behind the front plate of my body armour. It is time to get my head in the game and focus. Like so many soldiers in so many wars, I pack up my troubles and put on a brave face.

Leaving my room, I walk into the main area of the medical facility where the team are ready to go. Only Medic Matt is missing, his absence leaving a big gap in the team. I crank up the chirpiness and smile. "Right, come on. Let's do it, lads," I call. Moving out of the medical facility, we fit magazines to our rifles and make ready, chambering a round: ready to face whatever lies ahead.

We are halfway to Nipple Hill when we come under some initially ineffective bursts of enemy machine-gun fire. Counting the time between the snap of the bullets passing over my head and the subsequent thumping sound of the gun being fired (the bullets travel faster than sound), I work out that the enemy is about six hundred metres to our north. I surprise myself by my non-reaction to the gunfire and my rapid calculation.

As we carry on patrolling, the enemy fire becomes more accurate and persistent. We are on a ridgeline near Blue Pipe compound and have to take cover in some shallow depressions in the ground. Behind us, the Afghan platoon is putting down a huge amount of suppressive fire and one of their RPG men stands tall, silhouetted on the skyline while enthusiastically firing rocket after rocket towards the enemy. After a short while, Howard sends over a squad from the Afghan platoon to our position, to help form a firebase. While we wait for air support, the Afghans continue to fire at anything that moves. One of the guys from 11 Platoon is pleased to score a direct hit on a Taliban firing point with his 84-mm AT4 rocket launcher.

We now have an Apache attack helicopter with us, which begins suppressing the enemy with its missiles and gun. After a few minutes of this, the enemy should be keeping their heads down and we get the order to move. 11 Platoon is ordered to move towards the enemy. The execution of this simple order involves running down a four-hundred-metre exposed slope and dropping into the M4 wadi before pushing up onto the ridgeline beyond. As usual, I'm at the back end of the platoon when we set off to run down the hill.

Of all the things I've done so far on this tour, this is probably the craziest. No sooner have we set off running than the enemy fire intensifies; presumably the Taliban haven't got the message that they're supposed to be keeping their heads down. Unseen lumps of hot metal whizz past me on either side like angry hornets. Every now and then, bullets strike the ground near our feet to throw up plumes of dry earth from the hillside.

We all start off running in a zig-zag pattern. This method, known as hard targeting, is taught in training and is supposed to make it more difficult for someone to hit us. However, the incessant whizz of bullets flying towards us convinces me that I would be better off running straight ahead as fast as I can. As I stop zig-zagging and start to pelt down the hill as fast as possible, it is almost amusing to observe everyone else do the same. I console myself with the thought that nothing I am doing is new. My uncle served in Korea and my grandfather fought in the first world war; neither of them would be likely to think this action anything to write home about.

When we reach the relative safety of the wadi, we are just preparing to move up onto the next ridge when we're told that an A-10 is about to hit the enemy with an airstrike and we're too close to the impact zone. We have to run back up the hill down which we have just come. While we have been in the wadi, the Taliban have increased their rate of fire against the remaining call-signs on the hilltop; to run back up the hill now would be suicidal. We wait, therefore, for the fire support group to put down lots of suppressive fire before we move. The instant that the .50-calibre machine guns open up on the enemy, there is a perceptible slackening of the enemy's rate of fire and we move.

Running back up the hill is hideous. We are each carrying at least eighty pounds of equipment and cannot move quickly. The weight of our kit, combined with the steepness of the slope, means that we tire very quickly, struggling to reach the top of the hill in one continuous run. Despite the continued whip of bullets nearby, I'm not the only one who cannot help walking for a few paces near the top of the hill. It is almost miraculous that no one gets hit.

When we crest the hill, even the fittest guys are in tatters. 11 Platoon has a bit of a reorganisation and I find some cover to sit in. I share my little fold in the ground with a couple of the sappers. They are pissed off that they have not had the chance to blow anything up because this means they will have to walk back to base encumbered by their explosive charges, which are fashioned from anti-tank bar mines that have been sawn in half and are damned heavy. When the order comes to withdraw we carry out a hot extraction, which basically means that we jog for about a kilometre before walking the rest of the way home. Thankfully, we are cooled by a gentle breeze blowing northwards from the reservoir.

Our withdrawal is accompanied by some heavy-metal mood music in the form of repeated strafing runs by our American friend and his A-10. When the pilot goes off station, he radios JTAC Alex and says "Stay safe, brothers." Had we not experienced some pretty stiff fighting over the last few days, I would have regarded this comment from the pilot as somewhat contrived and cheesy. Now I take the message as it was presumably meant - heartfelt and sincere.

When we return to base I find that I have three surprise packages waiting for me. Our long-awaited medical resupply (not before time, considering the number of casualties we have treated recently), some mail from home, including an overdue birthday fruit cake from my parents, and Medic Matt's battle casualty replacement, a medic lance corporal named Sean. Phil has received a surprise gift, too. A Danish bomb disposal team, along with a British liaison officer, has arrived to do some mine clearance near the Kajaki dam. V volunteers to go with them as medical cover when they start the job tomorrow.

Shortly after our return from the patrol, we hear the unmistakable sound of an aircraft flying strafing runs further down the Helmand valley in the Kajaki Sofla area. JTAC Alex gets on his radio set in an attempt to speak to the pilot and find out who has sent him and what targets he is engaging. Alex cannot get through and after about twenty minutes the noise of the airstrike dies away, suggesting that the pilot is off-station.

Days later we discover that the airstrikes were being called in by a US special forces unit and that the attack has wounded a large number of civilians who turn up at another forward operating base to the south, causing a mass casualty incident. Gill, a colleague of mine, is instrumental in organising the triage, treatment and evacuation of these casualties, for which she is subsequently awarded a well-deserved Queen's Commendation for valuable service. For us, the most significant outcome of the attack is that the hospital at Camp Bastion is swamped by wounded civilians. With the operating room busy and no vacant intensive care beds, all planned patrols are cancelled. Phil is not happy.

The next few days sees the gradual consumption of my birthday fruit cake. I share it among my team and the military police with whom we share our accommodation. As there are a few slices left over, I give some to Pete and Phil who, it turns out, has also had a birthday recently. The company is joined by fire support group Delta, who take over the observation posts in the peaks for a while; this allows Phil to have an extra platoon on the ground. Until now, he has limited our operations to patrols of several hours duration which have been conducted mainly at night to avoid the scorching heat of the day. With more troops at his disposal for a limited period of time, Phil has decided to break out of this self-imposed restriction and put us on the ground for a longer period of time.

After a morning spent in preparation, we move out in the early afternoon and patrol down into Kajaki Olya. Whereas we have often pushed down the main road (Route 611), today we branch off early to infiltrate by hand-railing the river and using the wooded area of the green zone as cover. This route is intersected by numerous irrigation ditches and channels that are often crossed using rickety, improvised bridges fashioned from planks and fallen logs.

These crossings are sometimes precarious and no one wants to slip and fall into a stinking irrigation channel at the start of the operation. We make fairly rapid progress as we pass unopposed through the various compounds which previously indicated the forward line of enemy troops, going on to probe further south than ever before.

Our progress is aided by the use of a Royal Artillery unmanned aerial vehicle (UAV). The UAV resembles a large remote-controlled aeroplane with a camera attached to provide vertical reconnaissance. This enables us to be alert to the presence of enemy fighters. When the UAV flies over compounds to our south, we can hear the Taliban taking pot shots at it with their AKs, which leads us to suspect that it's only a matter of time before we get into a fight. As we are more likely to encounter resistance the further south we move, Phil instructs those platoons charged with clearance of the compounds to go in Red. This means that the men will fix bayonets to their rifles and post grenades into entry points, allowing them to explode before moving in with bursts of automatic fire to clear the compound.

Once again I am with 10 Platoon and patrolling with Steve, who has earned my respect by virtue of the stalwart leadership and immense courage under fire that he demonstrated in Mazdurak. As the sun begins its descent to the west we move from compound to compound, sometimes at a run, accompanied by the seemingly constant boom of exploding grenades and the chatter of automatic fire as the sections clear through about thirty metres ahead of us.

Every now and then, we get the opportunity for a pause and a swig of water while the next platoon echelons through our position to continue the clearance, like an armed game of leapfrog. On these occasions, I often get the chance to talk to the platoon commanders, their sergeants and the medics attached to their call-sign. So far, there are no combat casualties and nobody suffering from disease/non-battle injury (DNBI), meaning that from my perspective it's a good operation.

Wherever possible, we move from compound to compound using ditches and rat runs to avoid wandering along the main tracks and paths. Rather than entering compounds through the front door, we make use of existing breaches in the walls; if necessary, we make our own by employing the sappers and their mouse hole charges that are improvised with half a bar mine, some plastic explosive, a detonator and detonating cord, all held neatly together with duct tape. Each sapper carries four of these bad boys in their backpack on every patrol.

By sundown, we have almost cleared down as far as the east-west gridline on the map that Phil has earmarked as the limit of our exploitation for the entire operation. To avoid being ambushed at night by the enemy in his own backyard, Phil pulls us back to a temporary patrol base to spend the night at rest. The patrol base is a pair of compounds that sit in a defendable location. The CSM is there to greet us with a much-needed resupply of water and ammunition.

The compounds overlook a bend in the river which at this point is about one hundred metres across and flows lazily by. Our home for the night is littered with the remnants of a once-happy family life. A rusting pink child's bicycle sits outside, while long-faded family pictures litter the floor. One shows a handsome man in a suit and tie, while others are snapshots of a distant city complete with 1970s motor cars. I have no idea what city it is, but guess that it is somewhere in Pakistan. I wonder what might have happened the erstwhile inhabitants of our temporary base.

Did they escape from this unhappy land, or do their sun-bleached bones lie somewhere hereabouts? The heavy walls of the compound do not yield their secret and I shiver involuntarily at the thought.

We eat cold boil-in-the-bag ration-pack meals for supper and again at breakfast. The night passes without event, but none of us gets much sleep on the compound floor. I have a moment of pure panic when my wedding ring slips off my finger as I lay down my rifle. I scrabble about on the dusty floor searching for it to no avail. Fortunately, a second search using night-vision goggles and an infra-red light source brings success. As it is symbolic of my love for my wife, I fear that to lose my ring in this desolate corner of the world would be a portent of unhappy events and I'm relieved to find it.

Rising in the dark, we pack our kit in absolute silence, moving off before dawn. We retrace our steps and pick up the clearance where we left off the night before. Before long we reach the planned limit of exploitation, and Phil decides to continue further south in the hope of generating some activity.

As we move south the local civilians abandon their compounds, heading away from us. In one compound, despite the pleading of our interpreter, the occupants run away and leave their donkey behind along with a recently boiled pot of chai. The inhabitants have no reason to fear us and reports from other areas indicate that civilians usually vacate their homes when it is likely that a fight between NATO troops and the Taliban is about to break out. Of course, it might be that the locals are afraid of us, in which case we have no worries, but we have to assume that this means the Taliban are close at hand. Phil and his Tac group are just behind us and he shouts an order for someone to secure the donkey; if there is going to be a fight, we don't need a donkey running loose in the middle of it. The donkey is as valuable to these folk as a tractor to a farmer back home and we won't be popular if it is maimed or killed. Unfortunately, as soon as the nearest soldier tries to grab the beast it goes completely mental, hee-hawing and kicking out at anyone who comes close. The donkey then follows his owners, heading out of the compound and running south.

Soon after the donkey has escaped we are patrolling down to the next compound, which Phil has designated as 10 Platoon's final objective. As most of the platoon have already made it to the compound, only one section is still to move in, followed by myself and Steve, a young private soldier. The track on which we are walking runs north-south, and our destination compound lies slightly to the east at a track intersection. The east-west track is bordered on our side by a low wall and a furrowed field. The enemy choose a good moment to initiate contact. The section to our front has just negotiated the left turn at the track junction to move towards the compound and presents a perfect side-on target. The next group (us) is still in single file and cannot provide much in the way of supporting fire. When the attack comes, the enemy use machine-gun fire and a rocket-propelled grenade which, had they been more effective, would have annihilated the section. Fortunately, the RPG whooshes overhead and explodes in the furrowed field, while the machine-gun fire is aimed too high and the bullets crack overhead and whizz past us.

The men in the rifle section sprint to the safety of the compound; hot on their tails, Steve, the private and I continue along the track at a run. The enemy fire is now more accurate so, rather than running the risk of dashing directly into a wall of flying metal, we take the only safe option and head for the cover of the low wall. As we dash through the furrowed field towards the safety of the wall, I lose my footing on the uneven ground and trip, falling flat on my face. For a brief moment I'm dazed, the wind knocked out of me; my knee is throbbing and I'm enjoying a very close-up view of Afghanistan. With the bullets continuing to fly over my head, I regain my composure. Embarrassed at having fallen, I look up to consider how best to get into cover. There is only one option – crawling on all fours.

As I move to the cover of the wall, I look across at Steve, whose expression is one of relief. Having arrived safely at the wall, he turned to check on the rest of us and seeing me flat on my face, assumed that I had been hit. We laugh. The incoming fire doesn't slacken off, so we all crawl along in the lee of the wall until we're as close to the compound entrance as we can get. Steve gets on the radio to the troops inside the compound and instructs them to provide us with some suppressing fire. When our guys begin firing, that's our signal to stand up, vault over the wall and leg it to the compound. Steve calls out, "3,2,1… go!" As I rise up and perform the least graceful gymnastic display ever seen, followed by a sprint that would shame Usain Bolt, there is only one word screaming through my head: "Fuck!"

When we reach the safety of the compound, our relief at still being alive causes us to giggle hysterically for a few seconds; however, there is still work to do. One of 10 Platoon's sections is pinned down by fire in a neighbouring compound. The sappers blow a hole in the wall to allow them to move into our compound and Phil brings the full weight of available firepower to bear on the enemy. In addition to rifle, machine gun and 84-mm rockets fired from our positions, the enemy is subjected to heavy machine gun fire, mortar bombs and Javelin missiles from the fire support group. Steve insists that I stay out of harm's way and avoid the ramparts of the compound.

With most of the platoon up there, there wouldn't be much room for me anyway.

Phil's orders, given over the radio, are for 11 and 10 Platoons, who are both in contact, to withdraw one at a time, each platoon providing support to the other. 11 Platoon will move first, followed by 10 Platoon. Controlling 10 Platoon's battle, Steve and Sam ensure that plenty of suppressive fire is provided to cover 11 Platoon's extraction. Before this moment, both platoons were in a strong defensive position; they were occupying neighbouring compounds providing mutual support with a degree of all-round defence and depth support provided by 9 Platoon to our rear and our continued offensive action. With 11 Platoon's withdrawal, we are vulnerable to a flanking manoeuvre by the enemy and at risk of encirclement, should the Taliban realise that we're on our own in this compound and choose to exploit our situation. Once 11 Platoon has pulled back, we have to act quickly.

The main gate by which we entered the compound is now being hammered by enemy fire – to go out that way would mean almost certain death. Instead, the safest option is for our friends the sappers to blow an exit point in the wall on the furthest side from the enemy. The men on the ramparts keep the Taliban's heads down while the sappers prepare the charge; when the charge is ready, everyone comes down off the roof and gets into cover on the ground floor.

Taking cover myself, I close my eyes, stick my fingers into my ears and keep my lips open but my teeth gritted in anticipation of the explosion. The last measure is an attempt to limit the overpressure caused by the blast and prevent the ingress of dust into my airway. When the charge detonates, I can see the orange flash rip through the compound even with my eyes closed. When I open them again, the area is filled with a dense cloud of dust which covers us all from head to toe. As the smoke and dust clears, we make our way into the courtyard to make good our escape.

This compound has probably been home to generations of the same family for centuries, until this morning. The living area on the northern side of the compound has been turned to rubble, over which we now scramble before running the three hundred metres back across the furrowed field to join the remainder of the company in the escaped donkey compound. 10 Platoon makes it back without any casualties and, as we begin the long slog back to base, a fast jet pounds the enemy positions and thwarts any enemy attempt to follow up.

Having consistently pushed the enemy further south over a number of weeks, Phil has achieved his aims of confirming the location of the main enemy defensive positions and ensuring that the Taliban does not feel secure in them. The only drawback of pushing so far south is the need to walk a lot further on our patrols: it takes us the best part of two hours to make the return journey to Zeebrugge. The fast jet remains on station to cover our withdrawal but drops no more bombs, only performing a show of force by making dummy runs over likely enemy positions.

When I reach the medical facility, I am the last of my team to return from the patrol. As I walk in, I drop my kit and tell anyone who will listen that the firefight this morning was a bit too close for comfort. Sitting in a chair in the corner is the British liaison officer for the Danish mine clearance team, who has managed to injure himself. He tells me that I am the fourth person to walk through the door and voice such sentiments. We laugh.

Doctor Matt now has a race against time to sort himself

out and pack his kit; we have received word that he is leaving on a helicopter to return to Camp Bastion this afternoon, before heading south to Garmsir.

13: BREAKING UP THE TEAM

As planned, Doctor Matt leaves on the helicopter to be replaced by Clarence, who arrives on the same chopper on which Matt has departed. Like Matt before him, Clarence respects my position as the commander of the medical detachment and we soon forge an effective working relationship that is similar in tenor to the one I had with Matt. I've known Clarence for about nine months and we get on well together. He brings news of what has been going on in the wider UK medical group. I show Clarence around the camp, introducing him to the key personnel, before using the large map in the operations room to give him a ground brief and a short run-through of our recent operations and my outline concept of medical support.

The following day, the company mounts a patrol out to a place called Mirzee, a small settlement several kilometres east of Mazdurak. It's a long, hot and uneventful patrol that fails to encourage any enemy activity. While out on this manoeuvre, a mine is discovered in one of the wadis and Phil's Tac party come across the remains of an enemy fighter who appears to have been killed by one of our mortars in a previous battle. The mines threat is clearly not going to go away and there is much debate as to whether the mines are being actively placed by the Taliban, remain where they were sown by the Russians, or have migrated along the wadis over the winter months when these channels become shallow streams.

On our return from the patrol, we medics have some work to do. A young soldier has presented with acute abdominal pain which we suspect might be appendicitis, and our old friend, the stabbed Afghan policeman, has returned from Camp Bastion a few days ago and now needs his sutures removed. Although the man with abdominal pain requires urgent hospital-level assessment and treatment, we have difficulty in obtaining a medical evacuation for him because he is not a combat casualty. We are supposed to be able to provide a level of care that is broadly comparable to the NHS, but on this occasion, I guess we are hampered by the lack of available helicopters. Also, I don't think the medical liaison officer in the JOC quite realises the seriousness of the complications that can result from an inflamed appendix. After lots of phone calls backwards and forwards in which we argue our case, we finally manage to get the MERT helicopter activated. In the evening, Phil gives orders for an operation to take place tomorrow morning; we're going back to Mazdurak.

We leave Zeebrugge at 04.45 next morning and patrol out across the bridge. Instead of going into town and stirring things up like last time, Phil has opted to envelop the village from the high ground that sits to the south-west. 10 Platoon will be on the high ground to form a firebase and provide overwatch, while the fire support group will set up a line of tripod-mounted GPMGs in the sustained fire role in the vicinity of Blue Pipe compound (scene of the 300-metre dash of death, down the hill and back up again, a few days ago). 11 Platoon has the lucky task of conducting a clearance of Barikju in the hope of encouraging the enemy in the vicinity of Mazdurak to engage them, while 9 Platoon is to act as the company reserve. For this operation, I will be patrolling with 10 Platoon and Geordie with 11. Geordie is not overly impressed with being allocated to the platoon that is the bait in the trap.

As 10 Platoon occupies the high ground, they are spotted by some sharp-eyed sentries in Rizaji, a settlement close to Mazdurak. Within minutes we are coming under sustained small arms fire. 10 Platoon returns fire, initiating an exchange that will last for three hours. To our right, the Afghan platoon and their British mentors are also having a sharp exchange of fire. The plan of envelopment from the high ground is changed when Phil decides to move 11 Platoon from their clearance task to reinforce the Afghan troops.

10 Platoon is reinforced by a pair of WMIK Land Rovers from the fire support group, which adds to the firepower being poured onto the enemy positions in Rizaji and Mazdurak. After about thirty minutes, we also have some additional firepower through the arrival of a pair of fast jets. What ensues is more of a firepower demonstration than a firefight. Although our adversaries put up a fight, including mortaring 11 Platoon and our Afghan comrades, we are at a distinct advantage. From the fast jets, which identify the Taliban mortar crew and destroy them, down to our trained battle shots with optic sights, we hold all the aces. One of our sharp-shooters, armed with the old pattern L-96 sniper rifle, scores two confirmed kills; the ICOM chatter also appears to indicate that the company has inflicted significant casualties, including two commanders killed.

I do not rejoice in anyone's death, but we are professionals and the Taliban are our enemies. Far from being locals defending their hearth and home from western aggression, our interpreters who listen to the ICOM chatter tell us that our enemies are hard-core fighters from Pakistan who have come here with the express purpose of fighting us. Additionally, all the evidence that we have seen so far indicates that Mazdurak and the surrounding villages have been abandoned by their inhabitants, meaning that the only people we are likely to encounter out there are hostile.

If rumour is to be believed, some of our enemies have come from farther afield than Pakistan. Almost every British soldier serving in Helmand has heard the claim that Taliban commanders with English accents have been heard speaking on the ICOM, and that on one occasion a British patrol came across a dead fighter whose arm was emblazoned with a tattoo of Leeds United FC.

Rather than coming to an abrupt halt, the firefight ends when enemy resistance fizzles out and the company's supply of ammunition begins to dwindle. We move back off the high ground and begin the journey back to base. The challenges presented by this terrain are highlighted when one of the WMIK Land Rovers gets bogged down in the soft mud of the wadi. A second WMIK also becomes stuck while trying to effect a recovery, so the Pinzgauer is summoned to tow them both out. When the vehicles are freed they move to a vantage point to cover our withdrawal, overtaking us as we move back through Tangye and leaving us to suffer the leg-sapping climb up the hill into our base.

The following day I stay behind to man the medical facility while the rest of the team are on the ground, patrolling in and around the Chineh area. It becomes apparent that we are having a degree of success with our demanding schedule of patrols - as the company patrols out, they are spotted by Taliban observers. The interpreters report that the enemy are moaning to each other on the ICOM, complaining that we never seem to take a break from picking fights with them. It is reassuring to hear.

The patrol leads to a prolonged firefight near Chineh. From my position on the sofa in the medical facility I can hear the mortar line join the battle, firing high explosive at the enemy. As I sit there worrying about the men in contact, the building shakes with each outgoing round. After a while, I join Dave in the operations room to listen in to the battle on the radio net. I breathe my usual sigh of relief and send gratitude heavenwards when the company returns safe and sound with no casualties.

Geordie is grinning from ear to ear when he returns. The platoon he was with found a compound brimming with fully-grown cannabis plants. When the find was reported to higher headquarters, the instruction was to destroy them. Geordie was given the honour of doing so with a red phosphorus grenade. I don't ask him if he inhaled the smoke.

Once the company is back in, Phil tells me that there is some good news on the progress of some of the worst-injured casualties from the raid on Mazdurak. A, who was shot in the face, has regained consciousness and is doing well, although he has lost an eye. The other news is that Geordie will be leaving soon, to be replaced by another medic. This move comes sooner than expected.

In the afternoon, I am summoned to the operations room to take a call from Camp Bastion; the replacement medic is inbound on this afternoon's supply helicopter. Putting the phone down, I dash back to the medical facility. Geordie barely has time to pack and get on the transport to the helicopter landing site. We shake hands as I bid him farewell. A lot has happened in the seven weeks since we arrived together on the helicopter from Camp Bastion. Of my original three-man team, Matt is in hospital in the UK and Geordie is being redeployed elsewhere. It is a sad moment.

14 DON'T FORGET THE JOKER

In the days after Geordie's departure, the operational activity drops off; we have a couple of days without patrols to allow the company to rest after the frenetic activity of the last few days. I take advantage of the break to conduct some first-aid refresher training for the platoons and catch up on the routine administrative business of running a detachment. I complete the weekly medical situation report, which consists of an itemised list of the number of soldiers treated, the reason for treatment and any requests for medical resupply. I have an additional request this week: I ask for some board games, books and DVDs to be sent up to help relieve some of the boredom of downtime between patrols. The value of such creature comforts is immense, helping us to relax and feel a little more at home.

In the afternoon, Phil gives his commanders a warning order for a large-scale operation to clear the Taliban out of Kajaki Olya and Kajaki Sofla. The proposed plan is for a battle-group level operation, for which Phil asks me to prepare a medical plan. The enemy is well ensconced in Kajaki Sofla, a large village made up of numerous compounds. A cursory look at the aerial photographs leads me to the conclusion that, should the enemy choose to fight, the operation could make our raid on Mazdurak look like child's play. I set to work on my plan, working out how to best to provide medical support to Phil's outline operational plan. After several hours of working through the options, I produce what I believe is a workable scheme, which is submitted to battlegroup headquarters along with all of Phil's planning materials.

The following morning, Clarence and I are called to the OMLT compound to see Ricky, who has a high fever with abdominal cramps and is delirious. As one of the soldiers who went on pre-deployment training in Kenya, there is a possibility that Ricky might have malaria. We give him some IV fluids and paracetamol, and arrange his evacuation to Bastion. As the day wears on, Frankie falls ill with gastroenteritis, also needing a drip. I spend the day nursing the men, being as meticulous about my hand hygiene as possible; I really don't want to fall ill myself. In the evening I have some abdominal cramps, but convince myself that all will be fine.

I am wrong. After a terrible sleep accompanied by vivid and violent dreams, I awake at 02.00 with the most horrendous abdominal cramps imaginable. Grabbing my head-torch, I walk as swiftly as possible to the latrine while doing my best to keep my butt clenched. I make it in time, but can no longer deny that I have gastroenteritis. I spend the remainder of the night making the perilous dash betwixt bed and latrine until, dehydrated and washed out, my final action of the night is a long, sloppy baritone fart. One of the guys takes my turn on patrol, whilst I do my best to rehydrate and recover. By mid-afternoon I have improved a lot and decide that it's safe to try some food.

 I'm disappointed to have missed out on my patrol, another aggressive clearance of Chineh, intended to keep the enemy from infiltrating too close to the Kajaki dam. I find that I am increasingly taking on the more dangerous patrols, partly to show leadership to my new team members. I've no desire to become a casualty, but nor can I or will I use my rank and clinical qualification as an excuse for not exposing myself to the same danger as the men.

The next twenty-four hours sees all the medical team back on our feet in time to enjoy a volleyball competition, in recognition of the fact that today is F.A. cup final day, with Chelsea drawn to play against Manchester United. The original plan was for us to have a barbecue and for the signals detachment to set up a satellite feed that would enable the men to watch the match. Sadly, both plans fail; the first due to a lack of fresh meat, the second due to poor satellite reception. We make do with a Gurkha-style curry lunch instead.

At the evening briefing, Phil tells us that the big operation we were planning a few days ago has been shelved. As part of the ink spots strategy, there is a need for the enemy to be pushed back in all areas, however places such as the towns of Gereshk, Sangin, and Lashkar Gah are a higher priority at present and the resources needed to mount an operation on the scale that we planned are just not available at the moment. I am no General, but I reckon that to do a proper job of securing the Kajaki area and creating the conditions for normal life to thrive here would take a Battalion of soldiers – three times the number here at present. Throughout the early years of the Helmand campaign, force strengths fall well short of the numbers required to achieve the ratio of security forces personnel to civilians traditionally considered necessary to achieve success in a counterinsurgency campaign. It will not be until the addition of US Marines into Helmand in 2009 that force levels can lead to success on a larger scale.

After the briefing, I get a second piece of disappointing news; I am to be relocated back to Bastion in the next few days. Although this was planned as part of the scheduled rotation of medical personnel, it is still a kick in the nuts. I have developed a strong affinity for C Company and wish that I could remain with them for the duration of the tour. Despite my protests to our squadron commander in Bastion, the party line is that 'orders is orders'.

The next day, Phil briefs us that the company will be going back into Mazdurak for another clearance operation. Sean will remain at the medical facility, while Clarence will be in in the Pinzgauer as usual. This leaves me to cover 9 Platoon and V to patrol with 11 Platoon. I spend the day prepping my rifle and kit for battle and packing up my few belongings into my rucksack as I will be leaving Kajaki almost as soon as the company returns from the patrol.

C Company will be going out short-handed on this patrol, as the Afghan troops are refusing to soldier. Despite the best efforts of the OMLT team to keep them on track, the Afghan's frustration at months without pay has boiled over. It is common knowledge that corruption is widespread in Afghanistan's army. It is frequently claimed that their officers create units manned by ghost soldiers to embezzle money. The issue of non-payment has been raised many times, but as the army of a sovereign nation, there is little pressure that can be brought to bear by British commanders to remedy the situation. This means that Ricky's replacement, a reservist sergeant who is a paramedic in civilian life, who would usually be with the Afghans, will be patrolling with us as well. I have a wakeful night, due to brooding about my impending return to Bastion and the prospect of another patrol deep into the heart of Mazdurak. Although I pray that we have no more casualties, deep down I am sure this is a false hope; last time, we got off lightly with five men wounded.

There have been so many close calls and lucky escapes during my time in Kajaki that I sometimes believe we're being watched over by guardian angels. Although I pray that our luck will continue to hold, I cannot stop the verse from that old Motorhead song rolling through my thoughts. The last time I heard the song was when Medic Matt and I listened to it on his iPod the night before the raid on Mazdurak:

You know I'm born to lose,
And gambling's for fools,

But that's the way I like it baby,
I don't wanna live forever …
And don't forget the joker.

When my alarm sounds for reveille at 03.15, it feels as though I've hardly slept. I give Clarence a kick to let him know that it's time for him to rise and shine. Still half-dressed, I'm disturbed by an insistent thumping on the door of our medical facility. A pale, sweating soldier walks in; he reports that he's been suffering with diarrhoea and vomiting since the previous evening. Sean is already up but not going on patrol, so he takes care of the sick man while the rest of us get ready.

I'm already hungry and have that hollow, slightly nauseous feeling in my stomach which seems to accompany these early morning trips. I eat a block of oatmeal biscuit and a ration-pack chocolate bar to take the edge off the hunger pangs, throw on the rest of my kit and move outside with the other guys going on patrol. It's a routine that I've completed dozens of times before, but today it feels different: the sense of foreboding that dominated my thoughts through the night will not go away.

Our route out is almost identical to that which we followed on our first patrol into Mazdurak, almost three weeks ago. Just before dawn, we stop short in a holding point to the south-east of the village and wait, while the FSG gets into position on the ridgeline where 10 Platoon came under contact on our last abortive attempt at clearing this maze of half-demolished compounds. Phil has given the ridgeline a new title: Essex Ridge, named in honour of the county whose name C Company bears.

As the FSG moves up onto Essex Ridge, it provides a convenient target for any Taliban fighters who might be awake at this hour. The Land Rovers are silhouetted against the glow of the rising sun and soon come under some quite effective small-arms fire, which is quickly answered in kind by fire from the FSG's deadly arsenal. This exchange of fire gives Phil the opportunity to notify battlegroup headquarters that the TIC is open, and give JTAC Alex the order to call in the close air support that he has pre-ordered. It's time to spring the trap.

As the morning's firefight begins to warm up, the rattle of small arms and machine gun fire echoes across the landscape. While this is happening, along with the rest of the company I am lying prone in a shallow gully that lies about three hundred metres from the edge of Mazdurak. The message soon comes down the line that an airstrike will be going down in one minute's time. We count down the seconds on our watches and hunker down in anticipation of the impact. High above us, the sound of jet engines is the only indication of what's coming.

The airstrike comes in swiftly and with devastating accuracy. Four orange-red flashes erupt one after the other across the buildings to our front, followed moments later by the whomp and crash of the explosions. Menacing pillars of smoke and debris rise high into the sky above the village, sucked up into the atmosphere, before falling back to earth with a pattering sound as particles of brick dust and clods of soil land on our helmets. A triumphant roar erupts among the watching soldiers, but we don't long have the luxury of being spectators; shortly afterwards, Phil gives us the order to move in.

Preceded by a creeping barrage of mortar fire, we run across the open ground between the gully and the first compound in Mazdurak. I experience a strong sense of déjà vu when we move in through the very compounds in which I treated the wounded men during our last visit. Traversing the open ground without incoming fire provides a different perspective; the distances involved are considerably shorter than they seemed when we were being shot at.

As we pass through the village, it is clear that all the compounds have taken a battering in the intervening weeks. In the first one, the thick walls have been lowered in height by about one metre and are now dotted with holes large enough for a man to climb through. The second compound has received a more drastic makeover; once-proud walls have been destroyed and the alleyway in which I treated A and C no longer exists, replaced by a mound of rubble.

The company pushes into the heart of Mazdurak. With the Afghan platoon on strike, 9 and 11 Platoons are left to leapfrog through each other from one compound to the next with no reserve platoon for exploitation or back-up. As we move towards the northern end of the village, 9 Platoon occupies a compound overlooking a patch of open ground and promptly comes under withering fire from the north. One of the sections is pushed to the west to secure the platoon's left flank, only to be immediately engaged by enemy positions to the west near Khovalehebad and Pyramid Hill.

The noise within the compound is deafening. Jamie, the platoon sergeant, is firing his 51-m mortar and the section on the compound roof is blazing away at the enemy to our north with all available weapons. With no warning, a machine gunner opens fire from just above and behind me. I'm on the edge of the machine gun's muzzle blast; as the shockwaves and turbulence beat the back and top of my helmet, my ears are briefly filled with a high-pitched noise. Then I temporarily lose my sense of hearing, leaving me in a muffled, isolated world of my own.

Jamie brings me to my senses by tapping me on the shoulder. "There's a man down, sir!" he shouts. "What are the injuries?" I ask. The deafness is receding slightly, but I'm still very hard of hearing. Jamie grins and points to his ears. "You'll have to shout up, sir, I've gone fucking deaf!" he cries. I grin back and indicate the same. "So have I! What are the injuries?" I bellow, pressing my mouth as close to his ear as I can. "Don't know yet; the guys are trying to get to him," replies the sergeant.

I stand to one side, doing anything I can to clear my ears; this ranges from performing the Valsalva manoeuvre to sticking my fingers in my ears and pushing them in and out. The deafness improves slightly. Jamie returns with an update. "It's a gunshot wound to the head, sir," he tells me. "The lads can't bring him in; you'll have to go out and get him." When I ask Jamie to tell me where the casualty is, he leads me to a modest hole in the wall. "Through there," he tells me.

Looking through the hole in the wall, I can see remnants of a second wall and an archway standing proud, seemingly immune to the destruction that has laid the rest of the building to waste. About forty metres beyond the archway there are three soldiers in a bomb crater, one of them firing at the enemy while the second man is giving first aid to the third.

Reacting instinctively, I commit the most reckless act of my life. Ducking through the hole in the wall, I dart round the corner and, legs pumping furiously, sprint towards the casualty – my casualty. After I have covered about five paces with the world around me moving in slow-motion, I hear Jamie and others shouting for the men behind me to provide me with covering fire. The world speeds up again: I am now aware of the incoming bullets smashing the ground near my feet and whipping past me on either side, and relieved to sense the outgoing suppressive fire passing over my head. Before I can berate myself for being the biggest fucking idiot ever to sport the Queen's uniform, I have covered the open ground and crested the bomb crater.

My arrival in the crater means that all four of us have to squeeze up close to remain in cover. The wounded man has already had a field dressing applied by his comrades; he is conscious but in a lot of pain, and is starting to feel dizzy and disoriented. Lifting the field dressing, I have a look underneath, half expecting to find an open skull fracture. I am amazed at what I see: a livid graze runs along the side of the soldier's head just above his right ear, which has been nicked. I replace the dressing and check this seemingly-blessed man for other injuries, especially for bleeding or cerebral-spinal fluid leakage from his nose and ears. There is nothing.

As we work our way down the man's body, his friend Joe who is assisting me makes a miraculous find: wedged between the man's body armour and his back is the bullet that caused his wound. It looks as though the bullet struck the front of his helmet, ricocheted around the inside to hit the back of the helmet before dropping out and coming to rest harmlessly where we find it. This soldier is one very lucky man, and once again I have the feeling that someone must be watching over us.

Looking to my left I can see Pete, the CSM, indicating to me that he is ready to evacuate the wounded man on the trailer of his quad bike. Confirming that Joe has a red phosphorus grenade, I run through the plan. Joe will throw out the grenade, and once the smokescreen has built up we will lift the wounded man out of the crater and I will carry him across to the sergeant-major. The other man, whose name I think is Jonno, will provide covering fire.

When I give the word, Joe pops the smoke and launches it to the front and right of our position. It soon fizzes up to produce a good smokescreen that billows across the front of the crater, and I start to move my casualty. My plan is to shift him to the lip of the crater and then carry him across to Pete in a fireman's lift. So much for the plan: the lip is narrower and the slope steeper than I realized. I position my patient on the lip of the crater. To my horror, as I climb out preparatory to lifting him up he begins to roll away down the slope with a WTF look on his face. It is not a neat manoeuvre but it works.

The wounded man practically lands at Pete's feet with me tumbling after. We load the man onto the stretcher on Pete's quad trailer. Resembling a military version of Peter Fonda's character in *Easy Rider*, Pete rides off into the smoke and dust to deliver the wounded man to Clarence, who will monitor his progress and organise onward transport to the helicopter.

I work my way back round to the compound where 9 Platoon is still fighting the enemy. As our best exit point is now being smashed by enemy machine-gun fire and rocket-propelled grenades, it is decided that the safest option is to blow our way out with a mouse-hole charge. Once the charge is set, we all take cover. I'm in a cellar with Jamie and Tom, 9 Platoon's commander.

When the charge is blown, there's so much debris that it takes about a minute for the daylight to penetrate through the dust. I happen to breathe in just at the point of detonation, inhaling a lungful of mud-brick dust, and begin to wheeze and cough like an old man. Coupled with the lack of daylight, I am seized by the sensation that we have been buried alive and I have to fight to quell a sense of rising panic. Months later, I discover that Tom and Jamie experienced exactly the same feeling of pure terror.

When the dust clears, we exit the compound and move back through the village to our entry point, playing our game of platoon leap-frog all the way. On our return to camp I get cleaned up and finish packing, disturbed by a phone call from Camp Bastion asking me why a T3 (walking wounded) casualty has been evacuated as a T1, unnecessarily putting the helicopter at risk. I explain that not only does the injured man have a closed head injury caused by a high-velocity bullet and is at risk of significant complications, but he was witnessed being shot by the company sergeant-major who immediately radioed the casualty in as a T1. I am angry that someone sitting at a desk in Bastion has the temerity to question the judgement of the clinician on the ground, but dare not push the point as my critic outranks me.

In the afternoon Frankie and I fly back to Camp Bastion along with Joe (my fellow crater-dweller from this morning). Joe is going on R&R, but first intends to visit his wounded mate and give him the bullet that nearly killed him. On our arrival, we're surprised to discover that there is no transport to collect us from the helipad. After about fifteen minutes of phoning, I eventually get through to squadron headquarters and a Land Rover is sent to collect us. Having spent weeks on the very edge of the NATO footprint in Helmand, facing danger almost daily and with a very basic lifestyle, it seems almost surreal to be back in an environment with some home comforts. Tomorrow I will be able to get my uniform laundered and have a haircut. In the meantime, I am ready for a really good sleep.

15 OPERATION BATAKA

Life in Camp Bastion is very different to Kajaki. For the last seven weeks my routine has been dictated by Phil's patrol schedule which, by necessity, has been varied to avoid setting a predictable pattern, but is largely biased towards operations at night or in the early hours of the morning to beat the heat. In Bastion, the pattern of life is routine and based around meals and office hours. We tend to get up around 05.30, shave and shower before having breakfast and starting work at 07.00. The working day is broken up by lunch at midday and a long break of several hours at around 15.00 to go for a run or do a workout in the gym.

Those in Bastion for the duration of the tour need to keep on top of their fitness as the food served in the cookhouse is excellent, with plentiful items that I have come to regard as luxuries: ice cream, fresh fruit, fresh bread and real meat. I'm sure that without frequent gym visits many folk here would pile on the pounds. After evening meal, we return to work for the J2 (intelligence) update and the squadron commander's prayers (briefing). This last activity of the day is a nod to the fact that we are on operations, as is the practice of working a seven-day week, with some down-time on Sundays.

The other big difference is the bullshit that flies around. I am not referring to the expectation that professional soldiers wear smartly-pressed uniforms and shave every day; that is simply good standards. I am referring to the shocking petty rivalries and dick fights that play out between some officers for whom only heat and separation from family differentiates life here from their routine in barracks back home. Major X complains that Squadron Leader Y uses a Land Rover to drive to dinner instead of walking, Lieutenant A feels that he is being bullied by

Captain B, whilst rumours abound that the quartermaster's staff are keeping luxuries for themselves which ought to be sent to the men at the sharp end.

No doubt this is the kind of bullshit that has been flying around armies since long before Caesar crossed the Rubicon, and is to be expected in a large military camp that is home to so many egos. However, it seems bizarre and childish when placed in the context of the near-daily fighting in which C Company has been engaged. I also cannot rid myself of the feeling that some of my colleagues who never leave Camp Bastion are naively jealous of those of us who have been out on the ground.

During the course of my first day back in Bastion, I chance to meet an older colonel. A reservist officer, this distinguished gentleman is the neurosurgeon from the field hospital. We have a conversation in which he realises that I was involved the day before in the initial treatment of the soldier with the gunshot wound to the head. I'm very pleased when he tells me that sending the man in as a T1 patient was absolutely the right call to make; a CAT scan showed that the boy had cerebral contusions for which he has received surgery.

Sadly, there are plenty of reminders of the frequent firefights in which the infantry and their attached personnel are involved. While I am in Bastion, the MERT helicopter is scrambled almost daily, sometimes several times a day. On one occasion, I become quite animated when I overhear someone in the dinner queue complain that they had a night of broken sleep due to the helicopter landing all the time.

More poignant than the MERT missions are the ramp ceremonies. These are formal rites in which fallen comrades are borne in flag-draped coffins at slow march onto a waiting C-130 transport aircraft, and are attended by all personnel not on essential duties, who form up on parade to pay their respects. During my comparatively short stay in Bastion there are four such ceremonies and, with the exception of a military policeman killed in a helicopter crash, all of the fallen have been infantry private soldiers or lance corporals; each so very young.

By mid-June, the mercury is hitting 129 degrees and the air-conditioning in our tented accommodation fails frequently, leaving us very hot and irritable. My boss keeps me busy with some bits and pieces of nugatory staff work, so when I get the opportunity to go on an education course at the Theatre Education Centre in Kandahar, I jump at the chance.

The course is run by an education officer in conjunction with an academic from the Royal Military Sandhurst, and provides a welcome break from the Bastion bullshit. It is a pleasant change of scenery, although after a week of studying the application of force through the lens of Clausewitz's seminal work 'On War', I am ready to ditch the theory and return to some practical.

When I return to Bastion with the new information trying to push the old knowledge out of my brain, I find my wish granted - I am heading down south to Garmsir to provide support to Operation Bataka, a deliberate operation that will be conducted by Battlegroup South, led by Lieutenant Colonel Angus Watson of the light dragoons. Six months prior to our deployment, I was attached to the light dragoons for an exercise on Salisbury plain in Wiltshire. It will be good to see them again. Accompanying me for the operation is Jase, a medic sergeant who is an old friend; we last worked together when I was a corporal and he was a private. As fellow Londoners, Jase and I have always got on well. The change in rank does not appear to have altered this.

When I phone home and tell my wife that I am going back out on the ground, she is very concerned for my safety. I do my best to reassure her, but as I haven't convinced myself, I doubt that I've convinced her either. As Jase and I are driven to the helipad to catch our flight, we're both lost in thought and neither of us says very much.

The Chinook flight from Bastion to Garmsir takes about forty minutes, much of it spent flying at high altitude to avoid direct fire from the ground. As we approach the landing site the pilot brings us in low and fast, hugging the terrain. Although we do not know it at the time, one of our Apache attack helicopter escorts is actually hit by small-arms fire and has to turn back to Bastion.

The landing site is situated a couple of kilometres from the base, out in the Helmand desert. When we arrive, as well as getting our own kit off the helicopter we have to unload the resupply for the base. The supplies, mail sacks, rations and lots of ammunition are stacked as neatly as we can manage; then we lie down on top of it all to prevent any loose or lightweight items being blown away by the downwash from this twin-rotor beast of burden. Should anything fly away, it could cause injury to one of us or serious damage to the helicopter. Soon after the chopper has departed, we load our equipment and the stores onto a waiting truck and climb on board for the fifteen-minute drive to the base. As we drive along a road that borders the Helmand river, we pass a few scattered compounds before arriving at the base.

Forward operating base Delhi, known as the FOB, has been home to a Number Three company of the Grenadier guards since the beginning of the tour. The Grenadiers are known throughout the world for their habit of dressing in scarlet tunics and standing guard outside some of Britain's historic palaces and castles. What many tourists do not appreciate is that, far from being chocolate-box ceremonial soldiers, the Grenadiers have an impressive history dating back more than three hundred years and a sterling reputation as fighting soldiers with battle honours including the wars of the Spanish and Austrian successions, the Napoleonic wars, the Crimea, both world wars, the Gulf war and Iraq. As with the Vikings in Kajaki and my time working in support of the parachute regiment in Sierra Leone, it will be an honour to serve alongside and care for the men of yet another distinguished regiment.

Doctor Matt has been here for several weeks and our roles are now reversed; his place as the medical commander is well established and he has fostered good relationships with the company commander, platoon commanders and platoon sergeants. I reciprocate the courtesy that he extended to me when he first arrived at Kajaki; despite having seniority in time served, I don't tread on his toes or undermine his position.

Already a lean man, Matt has lost more weight since I last saw him and looks gaunt compared to the well-fed faces of the Bastion crowd. Due to the lack of available water for washing and shaving, like all the soldiers here Matt has grown a beard. In his case, it is a hideously bushy ginger affair that makes him looks like a wild man of the mountains. Matt shows me around the small base and introduces me to the other officers. Among the new faces, I find a familiar one, the company sergeant-major, whom I first met on a training exercise in Norway seven years previously. It's good to see him and he greets me as an old friend.

The medical facility is very rudimentary and considerably smaller than the superior accommodation we had at

Kajaki. Despite the floor being regularly swept, the floor is constantly covered in sand, coupled with which the room is boiling hot even by Afghan standards. Considering that the Grenadiers are renowned for their smartness on parade and a degree of formality that might be considered antiquated by modern military standards, the routine in the FOB is relaxed. Everyone in the base stands to at dawn and dusk, but apart from that our time is mainly our own. As well as a good selection of books, there is an improvised gym which provides an opportunity to give unexercised muscles a bit of a work-out. As one cannot spend all day working out I spend much time devouring the books, feeding brain as well as brawn.

Over the course of our first few days at the FOB, the population grows in preparation for the operation; this puts a strain on the FOB's infrastructure. In addition to the Grenadiers, the added population at the FOB includes A company from the Worcestershire and Foresters regiment and a Royal Engineers troop. A few days before the start of the operation a combat logistic patrol pulls into the base, delivering a large resupply. The combat logistic patrol is a large convoy of big trucks laden with supplies, accompanied by a fleet of WMIK Land Rovers which provide force protection. While the slow-moving heavy vehicles make their journey across the deserts and tracks from Camp Bastion, the WMIKS constantly move around the convoy like sheepdogs, working to protect them from attack. This concept is known as fighting the logistics.

In addition to the troops, a news team from the BBC is now present, including the reporter Alistair Leithead and a cameraman. There is also an army combat camera team, which consists of military personnel trained as photographers who are armed and able to go into 'high threat' areas where civilian journos fear to tread. The photographs and footage they take are mainly for the military media publications, but may also be used by civilian news outlets. Leithead is very personable and takes time to talk to all of us. As he is a familiar face from TV and has a similar background to many officers, I have to remind myself that Leithead is not one of us and be mindful of what I say to him; there is always a risk of letting slip some sensitive information that might find its way into a news report. Military law forbids us from making unauthorised disclosures to the media and I don't want to inadvertently land myself in hot water.

Over the next couple of days, the plan for the operation takes shape and we eventually receive a full set of orders which are reinforced by practical and theoretical rehearsals. The latter are conducted using an impressive briefing model built out of stones and mud. The main purpose of the operation is to create the necessary conditions for the building of a bridge across a canal; this bridge will then enable coalition forces to move into and dominate an area currently controlled by the Taliban.

In order for the engineers to build their bridge, A Company will infiltrate by night, use infantry footbridges to establish a crossing point and then act as the covering force. Number Three Company will then conduct a forward passage of lines, crossing the canal to assault a number of Taliban positions known as Objective Scotch. This assault is designed to disrupt enemy activity while the bridge is being built. After the assault, Number Three Company will then conduct rearward passage of lines, withdrawing through the bridgehead. When this has taken place, all troops will return to the FOB. The whole operation will be initiated with a preliminary bombardment of the enemy positions by the Royal Artillery's 105-mm light guns which are based at FOB Dwyer, about ten kilometres away.

At the conclusion of the operation the Grenadiers will leave, to be replaced by A Company. The good news is that we will return to Bastion with the Grenadiers. After only a few days I am getting the Garmsir look, with the beginnings of a good beard, although I cannot compete with Matt, who looks like a ginger version of Osama bin Laden. Facial hair is not an issue; not being able to wash or shower is of much more concern.

The increase in population means that water is extremely scarce; we are therefore rationed to a solar-bag shower once every four days, cleaning ourselves with wet wipes in between. Within twenty-four hours of a shower, my body odour easily overpowers the fresh scent of the wet wipes. As it has become too humid to sleep inside the medical facility, we move our camp cots outside and sleep under the stars, ignoring the threat of mortar fire. To avoid skin conditions such as prickly heat, at night I strip off as much as possible to allow the air to get to my body. When I do, I smell bloody awful even to myself.

The day of the operation is a long time coming, causing both tension and boredom to mount. There is naturally a lot of work to be done in preparation, but the wait seems agonisingly long. After a final briefing, we move out to Checkpoint Balaklava, a football pitch-sized rectangle of double-height HESCO bastion, which serves as the assembly area for the operation. We get ourselves keyed up for the task, only to be told that it is postponed as there is a fault with the MERT helicopter, meaning that should a soldier be wounded, his evacuation by air to the field hospital might not be possible.

Following the postponement of the operation, we trudge back to FOB Delhi and settle down for the night. When one is psyched up for the operation, sleep doesn't come easily. To relax, Jase and I watch Sacha Baron Cohen's spoof documentary *Borat* on Matt's laptop. The humour in the movie is completely puerile, but has the effect of easing our tension. One of the scenes that amuses us most features Borat, a Kazakh TV presenter (played by Baron Cohen), speaking to an American lady who is holding a garage sale. Because the lady is selling goods at the roadside, Borat believes she is a gypsy whose tears can release him from a curse. Holding up a Barbie doll, Borat asks her, "Who is this lady you have shrunk? Was she the owner of this house that you have camped in front of?" Like overgrown schoolboys we repeat this quote, along with Borat's catchphrase, "Is nice!" laughing all the while.

The day of the operation passes in languid anticipation. The heat is intense to the point of being almost unbearable and even lounging around in the shade brings on perspiration. In the afternoon, some children report to the front gates of the FOB carrying a sickly-looking toddler. Matt assesses the little one, who looks liverish and slightly jaundiced. Because our training and equipment is designed to deal with trauma, life-threatening medical emergencies, minor illness and injuries, there's not a great deal that we can do aside from advising these children to take their sibling to the Bhost hospital in Laskhar Gah. Rooting through our ration packs, we give the older kids some water, boiled sweets and fruit biscuits. I wonder whether giving these kids British Army rations might turn them against us; if that doesn't, I can't imagine what would.

The next evening sees us back at Checkpoint Balaklava. Here we help Henry, the doctor with A Company 1 WFR, to set up a treatment bay that will serve as a trauma resuscitation facility to which casualties will be taken before evacuation to Camp Bastion. Together with Jase and Sam, another medic, I will be moving forward in direct support of Number Three Company for the assault and clearance of Objective Scotch. Matt and G, another medic, will be on hand to extract any casualties by vehicle from the breaching point into Objective Scotch.

Shortly before dusk, the 105-mm light guns carry out a preliminary bombardment of the Taliban positions. I have never before witnessed a live artillery barrage and the results are impressive, with salvo after salvo landing on the target area, which is soon obscured by smoke and dust. While the enemy's heads are kept down by the artillery, A Company moves off with their infantry footbridges to establish the bridgehead. The sappers follow behind them, ready to start the erection of their medium girder bridge, the first time that the Royal Engineers have built a bridge in combat operations since the Malaya emergency of the 1950s.

With the successful initiation of the first phase of the operation, there is not much to do except sit and wait. Sam, Jase and I grab some real estate and, after taking some happy snaps, stretch out on the ground and have a few hours' sleep. We are moving off at 03.00.

Today there is no need for an alarm clock. I wake at 02.30, pack my kit and relax for fifteen minutes before waking the others. We meet up with the company sergeant-major's party and head off in single file across some fields to the rendezvous point. It is a moonless night and keeping tabs with the man to one's front and rear requires a concerted effort. When we reach the rendezvous, only Sam is behind me. I start to worry. Fortunately, Jase appears about twenty seconds later with the rest of the company sergeant-major's party. Having become disoriented in the dark, Jase has brought his group to the rendezvous by a slightly circuitous route.

Each man is carrying a ridiculous weight of kit, consisting of the body armour we are wearing and the spare ammunition and medical supplies. Even at this time of night, the heat has not lessened and the exertion of loadbearing over even ground brings us out in a heavy sweat. Before Afghanistan, I was never aware that I have sweat glands around my eyes.

Before we reach the canal, there are a number of ditches to be crossed using the infantry footbridges placed by A Company. This is child's play. Then we arrive at the canal itself, which is traversed using several infantry footbridges that have been lashed together. As we cross, the bridge sways to and fro, the overlapped ends of each individual section moving against each other with every step. Even though it is not a steep drop into the canal, to fall would probably mean a broken leg for the unfortunate victim. I use the handrail to steady myself all the way across and make the far bank with a sense of relief. Once we are over we join Number Three Company, assembled in herringbone formation, the company commander awaiting confirmation that the last man has made it across the bridge.

Once the last man is in, the whispered message is passed up the line and after a short pause we move off. The forward passage of lines through A Company's position passes without problem, although the two ammo men in the company sergeant-major's party have difficulty maintaining the set pace due to the colossal loads that they carry. It is reported that, despite starting the operation with at least three litres each of drinking water, men are dehydrating so rapidly and drinking so much to compensate that they're already running out of water. When Number Three Company occupies the line of departure for its attack, a very quick water replenishment is provided. With thirty minutes to wait before H-hour, there is a chance for a brief rest.

The combat camera team and the BBC crew are just behind the medical team in the order of march, which means that we feature heavily in some of the still and video footage of the operation. However, when the report airs on BBC news, the only footage to make the cut is an unflattering view of my backside as I make my way through a compound entrance. While we are waiting, the sappers prepare demolition charges that will be used to blow down some compound walls to form a breach, through which casualties can be passed to a waiting vehicle instead of being carried on foot.

At 05.00, the operation begins in earnest with the lead platoon conducting its break-in battle. Within seconds the rattle of small-arms fire fills the air, along with the muffled thud of grenade explosions contained by metre-thick mud brick walls. Within each platoon the sections leapfrog each other to secure their objective, before the next platoon moves through to repeat the process again. In relative safety at the rear of the company, we move forward compound by compound like a caterpillar. As we cross a stretch of open ground to the second compound, the demolition charges are blown.

Arriving into the second compound, we are just in time to see the lead section launching its assault on the third compound. The section goes in red, using grenades to kill and stun any waiting enemy before moving in, firing bursts of automatic fire. We stay put here, with men posted to guard the entrances. All that Jase, Sam and I have to do is prepare to treat any wounded.

While we wait, the engineers explosive ordnance demolition team is busy checking some weapons left behind by the enemy to make sure they haven't been booby-trapped. Just beyond our compound lies the body of a dead Taliban fighter, killed by one of the assaulting sections. Because there is a concern that the dead man may be wearing an un-triggered suicide device, a rope line is tied around his wrist and the body dragged into our compound for a search, which reveals no such device.

While we are in the compound, a combination of attack helicopter, fast jet and artillery support is used to suppress depth positions to which the enemy have already withdrawn. As this is happening, Jase and I wander over to where the dead Taliban fighter lies to have a look at him. I can't explain why we do this; neither of us is a stranger to dead bodies, so it's more than mere morbid fascination. It may be because our adversaries are seldom seen alive and when they are, have a tendency not to stay alive for very long.

The dead man looks like he was in his mid-thirties, and is dressed in blue-grey shalwar kameez. I wonder what kind of person he was and what events in his life have led him here, lying limp and lifeless on the dusty ground in front of me in an obscure corner of Afghanistan. Was this his home ground, or had he come from elsewhere to fight us? Does he have a widow and fatherless children who have no idea he is dead and will only guess his fate when he fails to return home at the end of the summer fighting season? These questions will never be answered. He made his choices, as we have made ours, and today his luck ran out.

Another time, it may be my unlucky day; if I am unfortunate, one of his comrades might look down at me and wonder how I have come to such a pass. If I am really unlucky, I might remain alive long enough to experience brutal torture before death. I think of the compound in Kajaki Sofla known as French Doors, so called because of the tricolour daubed at its entrance. Rumour has it that this was the scene of a grisly episode in which members of a French special forces unit were captured by the Taliban and disembowelled while still alive, before eventually being killed with their own weapons. The story goes that the Taliban painted the colours of the French flag on the doors as a warning. I have no idea if the story is true, it could be a military myth, but it certainly fits with our enemy's reputation. Not for the first time since arriving in Afghanistan, that old verse of Kipling's bounces through my head.

Looking at the wounds that killed the fighter, I can identify grenade fragments and bullet wounds, indicating that he was killed by one of the soldiers on the ground this morning and not in last night's artillery strike. The dead man's spine is completely broken, which has left him lying folded in half with his feet behind his head at a grotesquely impossible angle. The scene is so unspeakably horrid that Jase and I resort to some very black humour, mimicking Borat.

"Gipsy, what have you been doing?" I begin, "Why are you folded in half, gipsy?" Jase laughs and responds with, "In my country, we lie down with our feet behind our head … is nice." "Nice!" I reply in my best faux Borat accent.

I have no idea where such poor taste in humour comes from, but it dispels the fear and emotion from the situation and I remind myself that today is not a day for normal behaviour.

The Borat conversation peters out and Jase lights a cigarette. Since today is not a normal day, when Jase offers me one, I accept. We stand in silence and smoke, staring at the dead man. Shortly afterwards, the word comes down that we are leaving. The body is left for the Taliban to deal with in accordance with the requirements of Islam which dictate that he must be buried before sunset.

We leapfrog back to the line of departure, my medical team, along with the combat camera team, taking turns to cover the movement of others, weapons poised and moving in our turn. Throughout the withdrawal, the fast jets and artillery continue to pound the enemy in depth as we walk back to Checkpoint Balaklava. When we reach the canal, we cross using the newly-built medium girder bridge. Number Three Company has achieved its aim of disrupting any Taliban activity that could have threatened the construction of the bridge and the operation has been completed without a single coalition casualty. It is a successful mission.

Dog-tired from our night's work, we trudge back into base and begin to sort out our lives. The plan is still for us to leave Garmsir with the Grenadiers, travelling in Viking armoured vehicles to FOB Dwyer, from which we will be extracted by helicopter the following day. The pressure on the FOB infrastructure means that a shower is out of the question, but I do manage to have a strip wash. When I return to the medical facility to start packing my kit, I'm greeted by the pungent smell of shit and the sound of a small child crying.

It is an unforgettable sight: two toddlers are laid on one of our stretchers. They have been slightly wounded in the bombardments of the morning. One infant is displaying the silent watchfulness typical of children that have experienced severe stress; the other is crying, visibly terrified and displaying the 'startle' reflex to each of the explosions that are taking place about two kilometres away but sound much closer. The building we're in shudders with each impact.

As well as our medical team, we have two female privates who accompanied the combat logistic patrol that arrived a couple of days ago. While we were out on the operation, these two soldiers maintained a presence in the medical facility and are ably treating the children under the guidance of Henry, the medical officer from 1 WFR. As there is nothing for me to do, I continue packing my kit rather than providing an unnecessary audience. A little later the children have been patched up and sent home, to come back in a day or two for review; their injuries are not sufficiently serious to warrant evacuation to the field hospital at Camp Bastion.

The soiled stretcher on which the children had lain serves as a reminder of the trauma that this building has witnessed. In the last thirteen years, I have served in seven warzones and realise that it is always the children who suffer the most. I think of my kids at home and how fortunate they are, compared to the innocents here who suffer for no other reason than being born in a country which has suffered near-constant conflict for three generations. I know that we take great care to avoid civilian casualties, but when so much firepower is deployed it is almost inevitable that some ordnance will land where it should not.

I cast my mind back to other children in other places: the girl in Sierra Leone whom we treated after she was shot while escaping from a gang of rebels who had raped her, the children in Iraq who laughed as they hurled stones at our Land Rovers, the lame boy in the wheelchair with no hands because someone suspected he might cast a vote against them in the future. What hope is there for these children? No schmaltzy Coca-Cola 'we are the world' vibe going on here - just more violence and another generation ready to take up arms where their fathers left off.

During the course of the previous night's operation and our early morning attack, despite drinking my fill of water I've become severely dehydrated. The punishing heat of the day makes matters worse and I am aware that I am losing the battle – my urine output is minimal and I'm constantly perspiring. The buildings offer some shade and I do my best to remain under cover as much as possible.

We have several false starts to our journey to FOB Dwyer and it is late afternoon by the time we head off in the Vikings. Four of us are crammed in the rear cab, along with all of our kit and equipment. It is a cramped and uncomfortable ride. The metal hull of the vehicle has been absorbing heat throughout the day; as we drive, the red orb of the sun slips over the horizon and the absorbed heat begins to radiate from the hull throughout the confines of the passenger compartment. The air-conditioning unit provides no relief.

By the time we arrive at Dwyer, it is pitch black. We disembark from our mobile sauna and are directed to set up bashas (simple tarpaulin shelters) in between two rows of Hesco Bastion. This material is made up of cuboid metal cages lined with hessian and filled with hardcore, rubble and sand to form a very effective protection against direct and indirect fire. We lay our sleeping bags out on the desert sand and sleep. I am becoming thirstier and chug back more water.

In the early hours of the morning, we are woken by the wind whistling through our little campsite and blowing half of the desert upon us. We are buried in a layer of fine sand that permeates every nook and cranny of our equipment and ourselves, but manage to return to sleep. Sunrise enables us to see the mess that the sandstorm has made – we look like a bedraggled bunch of failed Bedouin.

A morning briefing brings the unwelcome news that our extraction has been delayed for a further twenty-four hours. With nothing better to do than lie underneath our bashas, we kill the time by sleeping, reading or talking bollocks. We are running out of rations and one of the men pilfers some American ready-to-eat meals. The US rations are not to my taste, but I've been a soldier long enough to know that food is fuel and if you don't want to go hungry, you'd better eat.

By about 09.00, the heat is merciless and our makeshift shelters offer scant protection from the sun. Left with no choice but to lie on our roll mats, we strip to the waist and pull our trousers to our ankles in an attempt to allow air to circulate around our heat-stressed bodies. In the early afternoon, we are called to assist with a young guardsman who has collapsed with heat illness. We set up an IV and sponge him down with water, fanning him to reduce his temperature. When we get IV access, instead of a nice flow of liquid blood, the flashback into the cannula is a slow ooze of viscous crimson. The fluid resuscitation uses up our entire stock of IV bags.

As he becomes more hydrated the sick man becomes more responsive, but he is clearly in a bad way. A helicopter is summoned from Camp Bastion and, after an hour of toiling in the sun to revive him, we load the soldier onto a stretcher and hand him over to the MERT. Afterwards, I dawdle back to my basha to while away the rest of the day. I have a pounding headache and a tremendous thirst, despite frequent drinking. Because of treating the sick guardsman, we have missed the opportunity to replenish our water. By early evening I feel nauseous and begin to vomit intermittently I worry that I am losing the fight to maintain hydrated and that I will be carried from this base on a stretcher.

The following morning we have an early reveille. I have a light breakfast and keep taking sips in an attempt to rehydrate myself. By 09.00 we are lined up in sticks in the desert, outside the barbed wire perimeter of FOB Dwyer. We sit for about two hours in full combat dress, helmets and body armour waiting for a three-ship Chinook lift to take us back to Camp Bastion. Just as I begin to feel my brain is boiling, we finally hear the familiar sound of the helicopters in the distance which rises to a crescendo as they appear on the horizon, barely fifty metres above ground level.

With great effort, we stand and heave our backpacks onto our shoulders. Feeling weak and unsteady on my feet, I find it requires focus and willpower to complete the short walk to the tail ramp without fainting. We squeeze into the fuselage, sitting on our kit, and in a matter of minutes are airborne. The nausea lingers, but at least we have some relief from the heat. I somehow manage to defeat the urge to blow chunks all over my colleagues throughout the thirty-minute flight.

Arriving at Camp Bastion, we are picked up by one of our drivers and make the short journey to our section of camp, Brydon Lines. Brydon Lines is named after Doctor William Brydon, reputedly the sole survivor of the British retreat from Kabul in 1842. It is a cluster of air-conditioned tents set out on either side of a pathway made of rubberized metal roller-track. In our absence, life in Bastion has carried on as usual. It is a Sunday afternoon and those members of the close-support medical squadron who are not deployed on the ground are playing volleyball and enjoying some alcohol-free beer. Our squadron commander offers us a near-beer each. Taking them, we go to our tent and start the process of post-operational personal administration: cleaning our rifles, our kit and then ourselves.

The non-alcoholic beverage is a drink too far and I start throwing up again. Alternating between performing my routine chores and dashing to the bathroom to puke, I manage to clean my rifle, have a shower and put my dirty laundry in for washing before I'm found out. I am behind one of our tents doing an excellent impersonation of the little girl in *The Exorcist* when I am caught by the hospital squadron infection control nursing officer, who frog-marches me directly to the emergency department.

Thankfully they are not busy and I am rapidly assessed and undergo a battery of diagnostic tests. A preliminary set of blood tests shows that, rather than being dehydrated, I have overcompensated for my fluid loss with too much water. I have hyponatremia, a low level of sodium in my blood, which explains the escalating thirst, nausea and vomiting.

The doctors' initial plan is to correct my low sodium with a fluid restriction. I tell them what I think of that and robustly explain that I could drink a swimming pool and feel agitated and aggressive. Fortunately, they decide that I do need fluids and that the best option is to give me IV saline with added potassium and allow me to take oral rehydration salts. I am admitted to a ward for a couple of days.

I share the ward with a couple of fellow Brits, an Afghan soldier and a five-year-old Afghan girl who was wounded by a coalition airstrike. She is a lively little thing with a captivating smile. Once again the impact of the war on the innocent is driven home to me.

After being released, I have about a week to convalesce. It takes this long for me to stop feeling weak and dizzy, by which time I am bored and ready to escape from the humdrum routine of life in Bastion. It is ironic that my hardest battle in Afghanistan has turned out to be with my own altered physiology. FOB Dwyer was a horrendous shithole and I pity the poor artillerymen who spend the bulk of their tour there.

16 WELCOME BACK - MAZDURAK TONIGHT!

Following my release from hospital, I am desperate to fully recover from the after-effects of the hyponatraemia. I still feel weak and unsteady on my feet, particularly if I stand up too quickly. I also harbour a desire to spend as little time in Camp Bastion as possible and get back out on the ground. If I had a choice in the matter, I would prefer to return to C Company. Failing that, I will be glad to deploy out anywhere, but preferably with one of the other companies of the Viking battlegroup.

Our squadron commander believes that by rotating troops in and out of locations every six to eight weeks, he's giving his people a break from the physical and emotional stresses of operations and therefore spending his human capital wisely. Field Marshal Slim famously described an individual's personal courage as being like a bank balance, stating that commanders must be wise to avoid pushing their people to the point at which they become overdrawn. It is this analogy that springs to my mind when I think of my boss's plans.

In practice, what seemed like an excellent idea in Aldershot has been undermined by the affinity that the medical personnel develop for the infantry sub-units which they support. As a professional officer, I will go where I'm sent and support whomever I'm ordered to. However, after our trial by fire in Mazdurak and Kajaki Sofla, my spirit belongs to C Company and I'm aware that similar sentiments have been voiced by others in the squadron.

Be that as it may, there are other reasons for moving personnel around the various locations in Helmand province. The need for people to go home for their well-earned two week period of rest and relaxation, compounded by the opening of a number of new patrol bases means that the manpower needs to be spread more thinly. As the tour continues, it is inevitable that commanders who have become used to a generous ratio of medical personnel to fighting troops will have to make do with reduced numbers of medics, potentially a hard sell.

While I am stuck in Bastion, Task Force Helmand suffers a string of fatalities; two Estonian soldiers and a British soldier are killed in separate attacks, followed a couple of days later by two more British deaths. In consequence, Op Minimise is in force for almost a week. The policy is necessary and appropriate, but it is still a nuisance to be denied the opportunity of phoning home or using the internet. Since notification of next-of-kin happens before any news is released, I've told my wife that if she sees a death reported on TV, she will know that it isn't me.

Two of the British soldiers are killed on consecutive days, one of which sees the highest number of casualties yet sustained in one day on our tour. On this day, the MERT helicopter flies no fewer than five sorties and the emergency department of the field hospital is in danger of being overwhelmed. Together with a colleague, I am asked to go and offer my assistance. When we arrive, the emergency department is preparing for an influx of casualties and we set to work drawing up intravenous antibiotics and other medications.

Among the wounded brought in are four of a five-man fire-team from 1 Royal Anglian, which was hit by a rocket-propelled grenade. As we're treating them, I marvel at their good fortune in being alive. We spend a busy couple of hours triaging and treating the casualties until the flow has abated and my colleague and I are permitted to leave. Walking back to our accommodation, we comment on the fact that not a single one of the hospital staff thanked us for our assistance.

For those of us in Bastion, the deaths mean more repatriation ceremonies. Regardless of regiment or nationality, the same respects are paid. One of the British soldiers killed was a sergeant from 19 Regiment, Royal Artillery – the Highland Gunners. The ceremony is made all the more poignant by the presence of a lone piper playing 'Highland Cathedral' and the haunting lament 'Flowers of the Forest'. Writing in my diary that evening, I comment that the worthiness of our cause in Afghanistan brings some value to the loss of these men, a point of view that I will come to question in later years.

Eight days after my release from hospital, I am reviewed by the senior medical officer at Camp Bastion who tells me that my blood results have improved sufficiently for me to be deployed on the ground again. Later that day, I receive some more welcome news: Clarence is due to go home for R-and-R, which means that I will be sent back to Kajaki to replace him. Going back to C Company and Kajaki is the best outcome I could have hoped for. I expected to be given twenty-four hours warning of my redeployment, so it is something of a surprise when I am ordered to move to the helipad within sixty minutes.

The flight up to Kajaki passes without event and I am met off the helicopter by Jamie, who greets me with a warm handshake and tells me that the company is mounting an operation into Mazdurak this evening. After a short wait, I am driven up to the medical facility. Because Clarence has left on the helicopter on which I arrived, I don't get a verbal handover; instead he has left me some notes. These are not all he has left – for reasons known only to himself, Clarence has given me a gift in the form of a hand grenade, sitting on the small table that serves as my writing desk. I assume that this is a joke, based on my reputation for being an enthusiastic soldier.. Unsure what to do with this dangerous little keepsake, I hand it over to one of the infantrymen who will no doubt make better use of it than I.

I quickly sort out my gear and prep for the impending patrol. While doing so, I discover that in my haste to pack I have left behind some of my little luxury items: books, photos of my family and the small New Testament and army prayer sheets that serve as my moral sustenance and spiritual crutch for my journey through danger. Whilst spirituality may seem at odds with my role, I do find comfort in trusting my safety to a higher authority and listening to that still small voice of calm that comes through loud and clear when all hell is breaking loose around me. Even if I have forgotten the luxuries, I have packed the essentials for war and am soon ready.

Compared with my last stroll down Mazdurak high street, the patrol is something of an anti-climax. Back in the role that I was previously able to relinquish upon the arrival of Doctor Matt, I now have the luxury of riding to war in the back of the Pinzgauer, along with the frustration and worry of not being close to the action. We move out to Essex Ridge where we park up on the reverse side of the ridge, out of sight and out of the line of fire from the enemy's positions in Mazdurak.

Having patrolled out in the late afternoon, nightfall sees all the platoons engaged by multiple firing points. A fast jet is on station which drops a couple of bombs on the enemy positions; the thunder-like crash of the impact shakes the ground and although we do not see the explosions, they ignite some vegetation on the far side of the hill, the glow of which illuminates the night sky. Phil breaks off the patrol and withdraws the company. With no friendly casualties, my med pack stays zipped shut and I endure a bumpy ride back to base. Despite my relief at there being no casualties, I confess to my diary that it was quite a dull patrol.

Apart from dealing with a few minor cases of illness, the next day is uneventful. We have been joined by some journalists, including a team from the New York Times and a British freelance photographer whose brother is a rifleman in 10 Platoon. The freelancer has managed to bag a special feature with *Arena* magazine which will contrast the two siblings' jobs and lifestyles.

Shortly before dusk, the monotony of the day's routine is broken by a sound that once heard is never forgotten. With no warning other than a split-second whoosh, an explosion rocks the base. The attack alarm sounds and everyone who is outside dashes into hard cover, donning body armour and helmets - everyone, that is, except the journos from the *New York Times*. One of the soldiers notices them still wandering around the base on a sight-seeing tour and calls to them, "Get under cover!" No response; the journalists carry on as though they are taking a Sunday stroll. The man raises his voice. "Get into cover!" Still no reaction. The third time he bellows. "Oi! Fuckin' *New York Times*, we're under attack. Get into fuckin' cover NOW!"

Finally the press get the message and take cover. I witness this from my vantage point at the entrance to the medical facility and since there's no indication of further attack, I dash across to the operations room to find out if there are any casualties. Dave, customary cigarette in hand, happily tells me that my services are not required. We discuss the impact, agreeing that it was most likely a 107-mm Chinese rocket. I quip that the Taliban must have heard of my return to Kajaki and want to get me, which raises a laugh.

As we are talking, the mortar line stirs into action. The observation posts behind the base have positively identified the firing point and are firing heavy machine guns and javelin missiles at the enemy. Soon the mortars join in, launching high-explosive bombs at the Taliban. Once again our ability to quickly bring airpower to bear means that in addition to the mortars, the enemy are also on the receiving end of strafing cannon fire and a smart bomb. No more rockets are fired that night. I get to bed about 21.00; reveille is at 02.00.

The following morning's patrol takes us back to the area around Chineh and Kovalehebad. I feel a little guilty riding in the Pinzgauer while the men go out on foot, but at least nobody can deny that I've taken on my fair share of hard work and risk. During my time in Bastion, I came to realise that in some quarters there is muted disapproval of my having done so; the reasoning is that, as the senior clinician, I should avoid exposing myself to risk to be able to do the most for any casualties. This is a point of view with which I don't fully agree.

The Pinzgauer trundles along behind the platoons, making tactical stops at several familiar points along the way, including Royal Crescent and Strip Wood, before its final location in Chineh. It's clear that C Company has successfully kept the enemy on his back foot since the heady days of April and May, as our location this morning is further north than we could have managed back then. That is not to say, however, that the Taliban are no longer up for a fight; within twenty minutes of our parking up, the familiar frisson jolts through my body as the village echoes with the rattle and roar of single shots and automatic fire.

We have been joined on this patrol by one of the young military policemen, who is somewhat jumpy. At one point, a rocket-propelled grenade whizzes overhead to explode harmlessly behind us over the M1 wadi; at this, the poor boy is absolutely terrified. I do my best to reassure him but without marked success.

As on so many other patrols, Phil has pre-ordered some fast jet support which has lurked over the horizon for a while; it now enters from stage left in the form of a pair of B1 bombers, which make some strafing and bombing runs on the enemy positions. After the aerial bombardment, the enemy desists from firing at us and Phil gives the orders to withdraw. Once back in the base, we have a de-briefing in which it emerges that after the bombings, the enemy were heard on the ICOM scanner requesting medical aid and reinforcements. It's been another hard day's night and after cleaning my rifle, I have a shower and get some sleep.

Some days later, I am relaxing in the medical facility when the liaison officer visits to tell me that a local electricity worker has been electrocuted. Once I've gathered the team together, we can only wait for the unfortunate chap to be brought to us. As we contemplate the main problems he is likely to present with, most of us expect potential cardiac complications and electrical burns. It takes about an hour for the worker to arrive in the back of a pick-up truck, and a cursory glance shows that he has a shortened and deformed left leg – a barn-door, mid-shaft femoral fracture. With deft and gentle movements, we move the electrician on to a stretcher and into the medical facility.

I send for an interpreter and get to work on the primary survey – it would be a mistake to focus on the fracture at the expense of checking for other potentially life-threatening injuries. Our man is complaining of neck pain, so we opt for full spinal immobilisation. His breathing is fine, but I am concerned by the fracture as a snapped femur can result in a large internal haemorrhage. The mechanism of injury also suggests that he could have pelvic injuries, another potential cause of hidden haemorrhage. Splinting his fracture and applying pelvic splinting will help relieve the pain and reduce blood loss, while gaining intravenous access will mean that we can replace some lost blood with fluid if need be.

We are fortunate that the man has a good blood pressure and a palpable radial pulse. Giving him some morphine and prophylactic anti-emetic medicine cheers him up a little. We are even more fortunate that the field hospital at Camp Bastion will accept him as a patient. Within one hour of his arrival at my little emergency room, we have him nicely packaged with adequate pain control and load him onto the MERT Chinook: all in a day's work.

The next few patrols pass without incident, apart from a young lad who develops an allergic reaction after being stung five times in the face by a wasp. When I am taken to the soldier, he has recovered spontaneously and is adamant that he is fit to continue the patrol. After a discussion with his platoon sergeant, I agree that the man can continue, but must patrol with the platoon sergeant and the accompanying medic.

A few days later, we mount up at first light, and drive out of base after the bulk of the company has begun patrolling on foot. These days I am mainly vehicle-based whilst my men patrol with the platoons. We follow behind the company at a distance of about half a mile, pausing at a series of rendezvous points for twenty minutes at a time before pushing forward again. This way, we remain out of the range of enemy small arms fire, yet stay close enough to drive forward to pick up any wounded. Viewed from above, the company must resemble a large camouflaged caterpillar inching its way down the road.

After hours of slogging through the network of irrigation channels, furrowed fields and close vegetation that forms the green zone bordering the Helmand river, the company finally makes contact with the Taliban, coming under fire from a couple of enemy defensive positions in mud-brick compounds. From our vantage point at the rendezvous, we watch the ambush unfold. The distant threatening hiss of a rocket-propelled grenade echoes across the valley, the tell-tale trail of smoke arcing over the top of a compound. Whilst the RPG would be ineffective against modern armoured vehicles, if used accurately in this unorthodox indirect fire role, it could easily take out an eight-man section with an airburst explosion, causing devastating head and neck trauma to anyone in close proximity.

Phil has adopted a tactic where he tends to allow the enemy to initiate contact before cueing up close air support to hammer them with; there never seems to be a shortage of US and British jets eager to provide us with air cover. A short while after the firefight begins, we hear the unmistakable sound of a fast jet high above us. Down in the valley, the first group of enemy are joined by their friends in depth positions putting down more machine-gun fire, the distant rattle of small arms carrying on the breeze. Bobby, our vehicle commander listens in on the company radio net and announces that the fast-air will be attacking in figures zero-two (two minutes).

I visualize how it must be for the lads in the forward positions. Any second now they will switch from engaging the enemy to keeping their heads down, praying that JTAC Alex has done his calculations correctly so that the pilot attacks the correct target As we count down the seconds, I stare at the second hand of my watch as it creeps around the dial, willing it to speed up. The pilot makes two runs at the compound, first strafing it with a cannon before making a second sortie to drop a couple of bombs.

The aircraft sweeps overhead, climbing out of its dive to leave behind a scene of hell on earth; the compound is momentarily engulfed in a series of bright explosions that transform into burgeoning palls of thick black smoke. The bombs are bang on target and we rejoice. The joy is twofold – it looks like we have hit the Taliban so hard that the gunfire has stopped and none of the boys in the company have been hit.

A short while later, Bobby tells us that Phil is drawing the patrol to a close. With enemy resistance having melted away, the company is going to check the compound that had just been bombed to conduct a quick battle damage assessment before heading back in to Zeebrugge. Moments later, Bobby receives another radio message informing us that we can head back to base, but must be ready to react to any emergencies.

When I get back to our base, I take the opportunity to remove my body armour. My sweat-soaked combat shirt clings to my torso and a film of perspiration, dust and salt crystals covers my body. I stink. Stripping to the waist, I sit on my camp cot and chug back a bottle of water that is almost hot enough to make tea with and contemplate the day's patrol.

I have mixed feelings about being vehicle-based. Now that I have a larger medical team, I no longer need to position myself so far forward and it does make sense for me to be the focal point for casualties being brought from the platoons. In some respects I am relieved at remaining comparatively safe. However, I do have a sense of guilt that stems from not sharing the burden of danger.

A series of hurried footsteps approaching the medical facility grabs my attention. It is Bobby.
"Sir, we've got to get back out on the ground; they've

found some casualties," he tells me.

"No problem," I call back. "I'm just coming."

I hurriedly dress myself, donning my sodden shirt which already feels cold and greasy against my skin.

Two minutes later, fully geared up, I am standing in the rear of the Pinzgauer, holding on tight as Bobby guns the engine and we head back down into Kajaki Sofla. A cloud of dust billows from the rear wheels which skid on the loose gravel surface of the road. Bobby almost loses the back end a couple of times, but we soon arrive safely at the bombed compound. As we approach, the men are milling around and there is clearly a bit of a flap on.

Phil gives me a quick briefing. He tells me that when the lead platoon cleared through the compound, they discovered that there had been a group of enemy inside the courtyard. Two of the four now lie dead, their bodies twisted at grotesque angles. The other two men had been occupying a bunker in the courtyard. Although the explosions caused the sides of the bunker to collapse, burying the men, their heads were clear of the loose mud that filled the trench and they are still alive. When I arrive, the Afghan national army platoon has dug the wounded Taliban out of the bunker. Miraculously, one of them is only lightly injured and is being cared for (and interrogated) by the men from the OMLT.

Ricky, the OMLT medic and I work together on the more severely injured casualty. I am amazed to find that, although he is unconscious, he is breathing spontaneously and has a radial pulse present. There is very little that I can do for this man in the field, so I opt to 'scoop and run'. We load the casualty onto a stretcher and place him on the Pinzgauer. Bobby drives us back to Zeebrugge with more care than he demonstrated on the way out. Arriving back, we take our casualty straight into the medical facility.

I set to work on stabilizing the patient, giving him oxygen and starting an IV as his radial pulse is weakening. Although he is unresponsive, I am convinced that the Talib is more alert than he is letting on. The interpreter, an Afghan civilian who faces the same risks as the soldiers, but with no means of self-defence, is summoned to try to speak to the wounded fighter, but the courage he displays in accompanying us on patrol does not extend to getting up close and personal with the Taliban and he refuses to be in the same room as him. The interpreter's reluctance is fully understandable; the Taliban would regard him as a collaborator and I can only begin to imagine the kind of retribution that he or his family could be subjected to. I remind myself that these people were here before us and are likely to remain here long after we have left. Sadly, this means that we have a patient with no name and scant clinical details. The MERT helicopter is already inbound from Camp Bastion; meaning that I have about thirty minutes in which to stabilise my patient, prepare him for transport and arrange for him to be moved to the helipad.

For the short trip to the helipad, we are joined by his more alert comrade who is clearly agitated by what he assumes is going to happen until he sees that we are providing medical care. We can hear the Chinook helicopter before we see it, the rotor blades making their distinct, instantly recognisable whopping sound. The helicopter flies in from behind the observation posts and touches down on the riverside landing site. The riskiest part of this manoeuvre is hovering over the river before gliding to the left to land on terra firma.

We wait to one side of the landing site in order to protect the patients from the mass of flying stones and debris that are kicked up by the powerful down-draft. Drowned out by the sound of the helicopter engines so that he will never hear me, I look down at the patient whose life I have saved, a man who I am sure would happily slit my throat, and very quietly vocalise the thought that has occupied my head since the moment I saw him. "How about that then, you fucking bastard?" I gloat. "I bet you didn't think this was going to happen when you woke up this morning, did you?"

Although nobody has heard me say it, I know that this is a thought that should have never been given vocal form and I immediately wish I could take it back. The more I am involved in this war, the more brutalised and less empathic I feel I have become. I wonder if my wife will recognise me when I finally get home, if I get home. Will I even recognise myself?

We load our patient on board and the helicopter is gone as quickly as it arrived. Afterwards I have a chat with Ricky. An impressive medic, later in the tour Ricky will demonstrate his mettle by treating casualties under fire, and take two bullets in the back plate of his body armour for doing so. Ricky is untroubled by the experience of digging out the severely-wounded Taliban. For my part, I'm untroubled by the experience of treating the casualties, but concerned because I'm not troubled.

A couple of nights later, a hammering on the front door of my medical facility-cum-accommodation rouses me to my senses. I check my watch, the luminescent dial gradually coming into focus as my eyes grow accustomed to being open. It is one o'clock in the morning. The sultry heat of the day has long since passed, but the plastered walls of our building continue to radiate the heat that they absorbed during the day. In a few weeks, it will become too hot to sleep inside the building and we will move our camp cots outdoors; opting for better sleep over the risk of indirect fire from the enemy.

As I rouse myself and stumble, sleep-drunk, to the front door, the hammering becomes louder and more urgent. I turn on the lights and make sure that the light trap (a black hessian curtain nailed to the inside of the doorframe to prevent white from light spilling out into the inky night) is in place. I open the door and a young soldier enters, dressed in camouflage shorts, flip-flops and a T-shirt. "Sir, there's a bloke been stung by a scorpion!" he cries.

"Don't worry, just get him to come and see me," I reply. A number of men in the company have been stung by various nasty critters in the last few weeks. Most have presented with mild symptoms and recovered with a dose of oral antihistamine and simple analgesia. I've become accustomed to treating such problems and have made the mistake of becoming a little blasé about them.

The soldier, a young lad that I recognise from several patrols, nods in agreement and rushes off, his slim frame disappearing into the gloom of the moonless night. Two minutes later he is back.
"Sir, he's in shit-state," he tells me.

Anxious to find out what 'shit-state' actually means, I grab my medical kit and a stretcher and tell the young squaddie to take me to his mate who is lying on a camp cot in a small, dark room adjacent to the operations room. The lights do not work in this room and I cannot make a decent assessment by torchlight. Scorpion-man, a young guardsman, is complaining of pain but doesn't seem severely affected. I try to get him to lie on the stretcher, but he refuses and says he will hop. Along with the young soldier, I help Scorpion-man to stand up and he tries to hop the thirty metres to the medical facility. As we walk, the unfortunate victim is clearly suffering and in considerable pain. I encourage him to keep going.

By the time we enter the well-lit medical facility, the patient is having difficulty standing. I look at him properly for the first time and am struck by the gravity of the situation. The soldier's face is marble-white, with beads of perspiration covering his forehead. This boy is going down big-style, and it is partially my fault for allowing him to attempt the walk to the medical facility.

Once we have manhandled the sick guardsman onto the stretcher, we lift it onto trestles so that he is at waist height and we can get to work. I order the other soldier to go into all the back rooms of the medical facility and wake my team up. He is gone only a matter of seconds, but the period of time that I'm alone with the casualty seems to last forever. I am trying to do several things at once to prevent the young soldier from dying. I grab the oxygen mask that is attached to the cylinder at the head of the stretcher, secure it to his face and turn on the oxygen to maximum flow rate. The patient, who I now know to be guardsman B, is starting to breathe noisily and tells me that his throat feels like it is closing up. I must act fast.

As soon as have I fitted the oxygen mask, I reach to the drugs tray on the shelf next to the stretcher and grab an epi-pen. This device looks like a magic marker; when the safety caps are removed and the business end placed against the patient's thigh, it launches a spring-loaded needle into the patient's skin and automatically administers a dose of epinephrine (adrenaline). I jab my patient with it.

This has taken about thirty seconds and I am now being joined by my medics, Adam and Charlie. I instruct Adam to get me a set of vital signs while I move onto the next intervention: gaining intravenous access. As Charlie prepares the IV kit, Adam reads out the blood pressure reading from the digital monitor; it is seventy over forty – one of the lowest I have ever recorded. A reading like that would usually prompt me to question the accuracy of the machine but, looking at the condition of my patient, I know it is spot-on. Guardsman B is suffering from severe shock and his peripheral vessels have begun to shut down, constricting to push what limited oxygenated blood is available to the heart and brain. I'm not convinced I can get an IV line into him, but must try. I choose a green cannula, about right for an average adult, and attempt to get IV access. It fails.

"Shit!" I think to myself, "There's no way I'm going to allow this boy to die!" Aware that it isn't the best option but deciding that it is my only chance, I grab a pink cannula, great for little old ladies in the medical admissions unit but generally scoffed at in military medicine. Tourniquet applied, I cannot see a vein so I close my eyes and palpate. I locate a decent vein, the tell-tale slight springiness giving it away. Exhaling and holding my breath like a sniper taking his shot, I insert the cannula. I feel the slight pop as the needle breaches the vein wall and blood flashes back into the chamber of the cannula. I advance the needle slightly into the vein and, holding it still, slide the plastic cannula into the vein. Releasing the tourniquet, I remove the needle, replacing it with the distal end of the IV line, which I screw into place on the hub of the cannula. Bingo! I tell Adam to smash through a 250-millilitre bolus of saline while I start prepping the next set of medications to give through the IV line. I push in chlorphenamine (an anti-histamine), hydrocortisone (a corticosteroid, to reduce the inflammatory response) and more epinephrine.

Chris, one of the military policemen who shares our accommodation joins us. I ask Chris to act as scribe and he does a sterling job, keeping an accurate record of actions taken, drugs administered and vital signs taken. Adam and Charlie are busy monitoring B's vital signs while I start running through the protocols to determine what medications to give next. Guardsman B is starting to rally, but is still very sick.

I have a bit of breathing space and realise that it is vital that we notify the joint operations command centre (JOCC) at Camp Bastion that we have a medical patient requiring urgent medical evacuation. I hurriedly scribble down a MIST report onto a piece of paper for Chris to take to the operations room. I am not at all convinced that our friends in the Royal Air Force will conduct a night time mission and prepare myself to care for the soldier until sunrise at the earliest. The guardsman needs to go to hospital, but if we must, we have the kit and expertise to look after him here for now.

The next hour is spent in a fight to maintain B in a stable condition as he swings between improvement and deterioration. We splint his legs to prevent further spread of the poison and I give repeat doses of epinephrine and hydrocortisone. Despite all that we're doing, B is complaining of pain in his legs and, most worryingly, severe chest pain. I administer IV morphine one milligram at a time until his pain diminishes. One of the side effects of morphine is severe nausea and vomiting. As I do not want a vomiting patient, I also administer an intravenous anti-emetic along with more chlorphenamine.

I am summoned to the Operations Room to give an update on B's condition and leave him in the care of Adam and Charlie. Still worried that the Air Force won't play, once I get on the phone I start to argue the case to escalate his priority for evacuation. I manage to convince the Medical Operations Desk at the JOCC of the seriousness of the situation and persuade them to send the MERT. Ironically enough, when I return to the medical facility, I find that B has rallied considerably and is looking much better. He has turned the corner.

At 03.00, we load a much-improved but still seriously ill B into the back of the Pinzgauer and drive slowly down to the landing site where he is picked up by a support helicopter. I am on an adrenaline buzz from having saved a man's life and dealing with such a challenging emergency. On the return trip from the helicopter landing site, I reflect on the night's work and think to myself that I might just have the best job in the world.

We bounce straight from handing over the care of B into battle prep and another patrol, this time down south into Kajaki Olya. Now that the adrenalin buzz has worn off, I am dog-tired and nauseous with fatigue. Fortunately the patrol passes without event and when I return to our base, I clean my rifle, have a shower and fall into a deep sleep until long after midday. I feel I've earned it.

A week after my return to Kajaki, the Vikings battlegroup begins to conduct a relocation of its rifle companies. Whilst 9 Platoon and the company headquarters platoon head off to Now Zad, the remainder of the company will soon move to a new location further down the Sangin Valley. Over the next few weeks, B Company will take over responsibility for Kajaki. Sadly, Pete, the stalwart company sergeant-major, will not be joining C Company in its new location as he is involved in an unfortunate accident a day or two before the move. For the sake of confidentiality, I cannot disclose the cause of or extent of his injuries, but Pete is taken by helicopter to Camp Bastion and then airlifted to Birmingham where he goes on to make a full recovery. He returns to Afghanistan before the end of the tour.

Before the balance of C Company departs, there is enough time for some more close calls. On one patrol to Mirzee, a pressure-plate improvised explosive device is discovered and detonated by the sappers and one of the sections from 11 Platoon has a very lucky escape when cannon fire from an A-10 strafing run comes perilously close to their positions.

Following the arrival of B Company, I take the time to get to know the company commander and the sergeant-major. Although I go out on a few patrols with B Company, the fact that I am not patrolling with the platoons inhibits my ability to form the close ties with the troops that I enjoyed with C Company. Shortly afterwards, I return to Bastion as it is finally my turn to go on R-and-R.

17 THE WAR AT HOME

It is mid-August and I have been away from Afghanistan for two weeks of rest and relaxation; a low-key affair, mainly spent with my family at our home in Aldershot. The excitement of returning home and seeing my loved ones is soon outweighed by the realisation that as soon as we've all got used to being together again, it will be time to pack my bags and go back to the war.

In the time that I've been away, my gorgeous son has made the transformation from baby to toddler; he is now walking and starting to talk as well. I could weep when I think of the moments that I have missed: his first birthday, for instance, the afternoon of which I spent sitting in a compound in Kajaki Olya with Steve and some other lads, with the angry spitting of machine-gun fire in the air and the whoosh of rocket-propelled grenades overhead – time I will never get back.

Whilst the nation pays my wage, soldiering and caring for wounded soldiers is my vocation, so I cannot and should not complain; I am still saddened, however, by the small sacrifice that my family has been required to make. I believe in the cause and feel that, if I finish my tour alive with limbs and sanity intact, the sacrifice will have been justified. The UK contribution to Afghanistan consists of about seven thousand personnel – each of them a father, husband, son, mother, wife or daughter. The fighting this summer has so far cost the lives of sixteen British soldiers, with considerably more wounded. The quality of the medical care in Afghanistan means that survival rates are higher than in any other conflict in the history of warfare, but the injuries that these young men and women will have to live with are more severe than those of their historic counterparts.

On the penultimate day of my time at home, BBC news announces the death of a soldier from 1 Royal Anglian. Although the name has not been released, the location of the incident convinces me that a solder from C Company has fallen. With a heavy heart, I dine with my wife, Lisa, at a local Italian restaurant that evening. The food is delicious and accompanied by a bottle of velvety, full-bodied red wine; it should charm my palate but I cannot enjoy it. The loss of a comrade has reminded me of what I am going back to and the risks that I face. With eight to ten weeks of the tour to run, I am not yet clear of the woods.

Yet again my mind lingers on a question that I have never satisfactorily answered. If you are going to die – whether it's pre-ordained or not – is it better to get hit at the start of the tour, in the middle or towards the end? I have made it to R-and-R; if I am killed before the end of the tour, at least I will have had a fortnight's respite from the battlefield, two weeks of family time. Many have not had that luxury. Private Chris Gray of A Company, 1 Royal Anglian was the first soldier killed on our tour; he fell on Friday 13th April, barely three weeks into the tour, his mother denied a final hug or the opportunity to say goodbye. Would it be any better to die towards the end of the period? Probably not – it would be an unbearably cruel stroke of fate to crush a family's hopes just when a joyful reunion is imminent. On balance, whatever stage of the tour it happens, dying is shit for all concerned.

When Lisa and I return home from the restaurant we make love, passionately confirming our mutual existence and reaffirming our love for one another. We embrace sleep as we each embrace the other, not wanting the night, our time together and our lives together to come to an end.

By midday of the following day, BBC news confirms the name of the soldier killed in action. My fears were justified

– it is a C Company soldier: Private Tony Rawson, twenty-seven years old, from Dagenham. I am wracked with guilt that I cannot put a face to the name. Then I see his picture on the television and instantly recognise one of the many unnamed faces that I have seen a thousand times, peering out from underneath the brim of a helmet, helping me drag a casualty to safety, warning me of danger, laughing with his friends in the dinner queue or while enjoying a game of volleyball during down-time. Tony may not have been a close friend, but he was certainly a comrade and I am touched by the sadness of his passing.

In my mind's eye, I can picture the scene: the frenzied extraction of a limp body to a place of safety, the subsequent struggle to locate the wounds and compress the bleeding, the fight to save a life and the bitter realisation that whatever one can do it is too little, too late in the face of devastating trauma. As the day wears on, the BBC website quotes excerpts from obituary notes penned by Dave Hicks. I am flying from RAF Brize Norton the following morning and have to report for transport from my barracks at silly o'clock.

Parting from Lisa is harder this time than at the beginning of the tour. All the way from Aldershot to Brize Norton I can still taste her kiss on my lips, feel her arms around me. I am protected. The flight takes off as scheduled and I sleep, read and listen to music, doing what I can to stave off the inevitable boredom. Hours later, sitting in helmets and body armour, we are ready to make the final approach to Kandahar Airfield when the pilot announces that, due to a technical hitch, we cannot land at Kandahar. Instead, we're diverted to Oman.

Landing at Muscat is a surreal experience. The plane taxis to a quiet corner of the airport where we wait for an age. When travelling with the Army, there are two mantras to remember: 'hurry up and wait' and 'on the bus, off the bus.' If you ever find yourself in the military of any nation, undertaking long-haul travel, just remember that you will always, always be fucked around.

Eventually a decision is made that we will not fly to Kandahar today. We are bussed to a five-star hotel complex outside Muscat where we will spend what's left of the night and most of the next day before completing our journey. This hotel is quite a fancy place. My commanding officer and I opt to share a room; opening the door, we find that, rather than twin beds, we have to share a king-size! We end up sleeping perched on opposite edges of the bed, resembling a scene from a farce. The heavy curtains keep the room darkened and we don't wake until midday. I later joke that I am the only captain to sleep with the colonel during his time in command.

I pity any other guests who have paid to stay at the hotel, be they ex-pat westerners or Gulf arabs. Their weekend has no doubt been ruined by the presence of about two hundred British soldiers who, in the absence of proper swimming attire, are splashing around wearing a variety of undergarments, ranging from army-issue pants to PT shorts. The colonel and I have a beer – the last we will enjoy for some time. I telephone home to speak with Lisa, who has some more bad news. The words are like a punch in the stomach, Lisa tells me that the Vikings have lost another soldier in Helmand, in the same place that Tony Rawson was killed. She thinks it is C Company again.

After an uneventful flight, we land at Kandahar in the early morning and are bussed to the transit accommodation; we won't fly on to Bastion until later that afternoon. At the transit tent, I bump into a sergeant from 1 Royal Anglian mortar platoon. We have a brief chat and I ask him if he knows anything about the latest casualty. It is not good news; as I listen, I can feel unwanted tears pricking at my eyes. Dave Hicks is dead. A man whom I have only known for a few months but grew to like immensely has fallen in battle.

In the days following my return from R&R, I am forced to endure several weeks in Camp Bastion. After the freedom of months spent bouncing around Helmand Province working in support of various units, Bastion feels like a very pleasant prison.

Over time it has become *de rigueur* for various senior officers, celebrities and public figures to come and visit troops in Afghanistan. During the limited time I have spent in Camp Bastion I have met or seen several of these VIP visitors, including Gordon Brown (chancellor of the exchequer), HRH the Duke of Gloucester and Ross Kemp (*Eastenders* actor turned documentary film-maker).

Gordon Brown wears a dark suit for the duration of his visit and, as far as I can tell, never leaves Bastion. I walk past him in the cookhouse where he is enjoying lunch with a group of specially-selected officers and soldiers, and manage to resist a strong puerile urge to accidentally-deliberately spill my cup of tea on him. I understand the need to host senior politicians, but feel a slight sense of outrage that the man who is tipped to become our future (unelected) prime minister will form an impression of Afghanistan based on the clean dining facilities, office spaces and operations rooms in Bastion and Lashkar Gah, as opposed to a fly-blown patrol base in which the men are on half-rations and a warm can of Coca-Cola is a luxury to be jealously guarded and hoarded for a special occasion.

As the colonel-in-chief of both the Royal Army Medical Corps and the Royal Anglian Regiment, the Duke of Gloucester visits the UK Joint Force Medical Group and

1 Royal Anglian. I am mildly amused that the duke manages to get closer to the action than some of our own officers.

Ross Kemp is producing a documentary about 1 Royal Anglian and has spent considerable time on operations with the battalion's B Company, earning the respect of the soldiers for his willingness to share the dangers of the frontline.

My time in Bastion has an unexpectedly pleasant surprise in the form of a visiting troupe from Combined Services Entertainment - the usual motley array of dancing girls, a risqué comedian and a rock band. The concert is held in a huge tent in the army air corps section of camp and goes down well with the troops. The rock band finishes the show with a cover version of the Metallica song 'Enter Sandman', their performance of which is made more popular by the artful deletion of the line 'We're off to Never-Never Land!' which is replaced by the equally poetic (and apt) 'We're off to kill the Taliban!'

Several days after my return from R&R, I am glad to have the opportunity to attend the repatriation ceremony for David Hicks and Tony Rawson. The ceremony is attended by almost the entire population of Camp Bastion and takes place in the late afternoon to reduce the likelihood of soldiers fainting in the heat. Everyone is dressed as though they're in barracks back home – belts on, shirts tucked in and berets worn. After a poignant service conducted by the battalion's chaplain, two bearer parties carry the Union Flag-draped coffins of our fallen comrades up the ramp into the belly of a Royal Air Force C-130 Hercules transport plane at slow march.

The bearers move the coffins with dignified precision, bodies erect, knees braced and toes pointed down, giving the appearance of gliding across the tarmac. The afternoon sun casts a golden glow over the scene as the aircraft gracefully taxies down the runway before turning to take off. The deep hum of the powerful propeller-engines rises to a crescendo and the plane takes off into the balmy sky, banking around to pass over the assembled troops below. The battalion's commanding officer and the regimental sergeant-major salute smartly as the C-130 passes overhead. The pilot dips the wings of the aircraft to return the compliment. I want to cry but I can't.

Despite the organised fun of Camp Bastion, I'm bored and just want to get back out on the ground. In the light of David's death, I am doing my damnedest to be sent to FOB Inkerman to be with C Company again. Instead, I am sent to Sangin to work in support of A Company.

18 SANGIN

Amid a volley of chaff and flares deployed to foil an enemy missile attack, our Chinook makes a rapid landing within the compound walls of the British base in Sangin. As the wheels hit the ground I'm already standing, rifle in my left hand. With my right hand, I lift the heavy backpack to mid-thigh. After a brief grapple with the cumbersome burden, I heave it onto my back, adjusting the straps to pull it in tight, the base wedged on the rearmost pouches of my belt kit. I am ready to go.

As the helicopter approaches ground level, the downwash from the rotor blades throws up a billowing cloud of brown dust that obscures the view beyond the tail ramp. Following the man in front I move to the rear of the helicopter and alight, much as a suited businessman in London steps off the Tube - except that businessmen do not carry 150lbs of kit on their backs, nor are they armed with a rifle and enough ammunition to start a small war. I have made my commute back to the front.

Sangin district centre (DC) is both remarkable and unremarkable at once. It looks like a fairly standard Afghan compound fortified with HESCO walls and sandbagged sentry positions, known as sangars. What makes Sangin remarkable is its reputation for being one of the most dangerous places on earth. Twelve months before our tour, Sangin DC was one of a number of platoon houses throughout Helmand province that were occupied by 3rd Battalion, the parachute regiment, as part of the move into the area. Dispersed in small numbers, the troops in each of these locations soon found themselves encircled and embattled.

As vital ground for both sides, the Taliban were never going to allow the Afghan government and its NATO allies to dominate this area without a fight, and the paras, with their well-deserved fighting reputation, were never going to take it lying down. As a consequence, Sangin has been a focal point for fighting during the previous twelve months, with a significant number of British soldiers killed in action here. Recently, however, a number of operations have pushed the enemy back from Sangin DC and restored a semblance of normality for its inhabitants.

My role in Sangin is simple: I have been brought in with a small group of medics to bolster the medical presence. The Vikings battlegroup is mounting another deliberate operation to extend the envelope of security further outwards from the town. Because the Vikings' doctor is deploying on the ground, I will be baby-sitting the medical facility in his absence.

I meet the doctor shortly after my arrival and find that we will be sharing the same accommodation – camp cots in a small partitioned space at the back of the medical facility. The medical facility itself is the usual affair, consisting of a couple of stretchers on trestles and Piggott pouches of medical equipment suspended from the walls.

The Piggott pouch consists of a large rectangular canvas base to which various pouches and bags have been sewn. It is arranged so that it can be folded in four and then closed with a zip like a suitcase. When closed, it is a little larger than a Bergen rucksack and can be carried using shoulder straps or a handle. The Piggott pouch contains the bulk of equipment required for a standard treatment bay module. In theory, this provides us with sufficient kit to treat up to ten major trauma cases; in practice, the number is realistically closer to two or three.

Despite damping the floor with water and a routine of daily sweeping and mopping, the fine dust of Afghanistan coats everything here and permeates all nooks and crannies. I lay my kit down on the spare camp cot and the doc, with whom I have worked several times in the past, gives me a guided tour of the base. Our accommodation is in the main building, which is a large house that must once have been a well-appointed des-res. This has a large reception hall and five or six sizeable rooms downstairs, a large basement which houses the ops room and a top floor with access to the roof. There is also a number of outbuildings, some of which serve as an isolation ward for soldiers with the misfortune to fall ill with diarrhoeal disease; while it can't quite be classed as an epidemic, this causes a couple of soldiers to be out of action on a fairly constant basis.

Also within the compound but separated by a couple of walls is an Afghan national army base. Between the separating walls runs a narrow but fast-flowing river, which is used by the troops for bathing and washing their uniforms. At times, it seems that the soldiers are having a competition to see how many men can fit into the river at the same time.

The resident chef provides a cooked dinner once a day from the field cooker located in the hall of the main house, whilst for breakfast and lunch we eat ration pack food. Each ration pack is a box containing enough food feed a man for twenty-four hours; some of the food comes in foil pouches that are heated by immersion in boiling water. The menu choices are limited, breakfast is usually baked beans with sausages or bacon and lunch is typically hard-baked biscuits with a tin of meat paste. Because the meat paste tends to go a bit yucky in the heat, we have been provided with a hot climate option of pre-cooked noodles and beef or pasta and tuna. Other concessions to the heat have been made, including providing us with muesli bars in place of the usual chocolate bars and sachets of isotonic sports drink. All the ration boxes are stored in a shipping container that sits in one corner of the base; we are trusted to help ourselves and not take more than our fair share.

As well as housing the kitchen, the entrance hall is also home to a large flat-screen TV with a Sky TV satellite service, which helps to kill time.

Dinner is served in the early evening and we take our food outside onto the terrace. The doctor introduces me to a correspondent and photographer from the 'Daily Telegraph'. The journo is a former army officer. Apart from his civilian attire he looks, talks and walks like one of us. As I did with Alistair Leithead, I remind myself that this man is loyal to nobody but his readers, his newspaper and himself. There is a real risk that he may use his familiarity to encourage us to make unauthorised disclosures to the media, with the potential result that our words can be taken out of context, manipulated or used against us.

As I make small talk with the news team, it emerges that the photographer and I are both from the same part of England and we have quite a chat about home; an amiable conversation with an amiable man. While we have been eating night has fallen rapidly, the short dusk bringing the day to an abrupt close. The doctor leaves to attend a briefing on the next operation, which is scheduled to start in thirty-six hours.

The following day is spent in preparation for this operation, which will involve the insertion of a large number of troops by helicopter to commence the clearance of the green zones, pushing northwards in the upper Sangin valley. This type of operation has been conducted all over Helmand this summer; although we defeat the Taliban in detail repeatedly, most of their fighters melt away only to re-infiltrate again later. As a result, we have to go back to the same places time and again to smash a different bunch of fighters there. Mowing the grass again.

Before our deployment, we were given a list of books that were regarded as essential pre-deployment reading. One of them, 'The Bear Went Over the Mountain', is a US translation of various accounts of Russian operations in Afghanistan. One of the vignettes, dated from the mid-1980s, is entitled 'Clearing a Green Zone in Helmand Province'. The basic premise of the account is depressingly familiar; delete the Soviet nomenclature of units, vehicles and weapon systems, insert our own and the story is the same. I fear we are merely repeating the follies of the Soviets and our own ancestors before us.

Aside from a few minor illnesses, things are relatively quiet in Sangin. At one point, an Afghan youth is brought to us. He has been accused by other street-kids of being a spy for the coalition and has been hit squarely in the eye with a brick. The doc and I examine the young lad's eye, improvising a saline irrigation from a bag of IV fluid and an administration set. Many nurses have an Achilles' heel, something that makes us want to vomit or faint despite the need to maintain a professional image. I have two; one is the crepitus of bone ends rubbing together whenever I realign a fractured leg for splinting, and the other is eyes. I administer the irrigation while the Doc examines the boy's eye. The lens is practically detached, hanging on by the loosest scrap of tissue. As I continue to irrigate, the tissue flap breaks and the lens is washed away on a tide of saline into the kidney dish that is held in place by one of the medics. I dry-retch, but manage to quell the nausea.

It is highly unlikely that this boy will have the use of that eye again. Because the injury was not caused by military action, we cannot refer him to the hospital in Camp Bastion. While I apply an eye patch, the doc writes a referral letter to the International Red Cross hospital in Kandahar. Our patient is given the letter and fifty US dollars, a king's ransom in Afghan terms, and advised to take a taxi to the hospital. None of us will ever know if he makes it.

Later that afternoon, I return from having a shower to find that the curtain is drawn across the entrance to the medical facility and a sign has been posted saying 'no entry, consultation in progress'. As I am medical staff and this is also my accommodation, I enter anyway. The doc is having a conversation with the correspondent. I don't know the full details of the conversation, but within a week there's a double-page spread in the *Telegraph* that bemoans the poor standard of medical support in Helmand. The article implies that inadequate medical support may have contributed to Dave's death. When I read this, I am incensed.

The two medics who were at FOB Inkerman were bloody good, on top of their game in every way. I know that they would have made every effort to save Dave's life and that the presence of a doctor would have made little difference to the outcome. Furthermore, the joint force medical group has consistently over-provided medical support throughout our tour of duty. Whilst it is great for morale, having nursing officers and doctors embedded at company level and medics at platoon level is well above the standard doctrinal provision of two medics per rifle company. Throughout the summer, the number of bases requiring medical support has increased, but the number of available medics has not; in fact, it has dwindled in real terms due to casualties and the need to rotate people home for R-and-R. I am convinced that the story must add to the burden of worry carried by all service families with loved ones serving in Afghanistan.

The following morning, the company deploys. The soldiers rise long before dawn and quietly make their way to the helicopter landing site. By first light, they have been picked up by several Chinooks and deposited at the drop-off point to begin the clearance. I have never enjoyed being left behind, but with the doctor out on the ground and the troops not from C Company, it bothers me less than usual. Throughout the day, we receive sporadic news of how the clearance is progressing. In the early evening, the troops are brought back by helicopter to Sangin DC and the doctor returns, bringing a patient.

The patient is a small child, about three years old. Towards the end of the day's clearance, the commanders held a shura (consultation) meeting with local elders. At the meeting this sickly child was presented, ostensibly with severe wounds that were allegedly caused by NATO forces. The doc did not have the opportunity to conduct a full examination at the shura, so to gain favour with the elders the decision was made that the child and her grandfather should be brought in for assessment and treatment. Only now does the doctor make a full examination, here in Sangin HQ.

As well as having an old fracture of the pelvis and lower back, the child is doubly incontinent, has extensive pressure sores that are badly infected and looks dehydrated and wizened; she is clearly failing to thrive. The injuries are at odds with the story that was told at the shura meeting and I am not convinced that we will have a solid case for her admittance to the Camp Bastion field hospital.

While the doc speaks to the med ops desk in the joint operations centre, I tend to the child's wounds, cleaning them with saline and removing slough and dead tissue.

Some of the pressure sores are almost full thickness and as I cleanse them with a gloved hand and saline-soaked gauze, I can feel bone immediately beneath the deeper surfaces. As I work, this poor girl is making the most heart-breaking sounds of anguish, more like the mewling of a kitten than the cry of a child. Once I have finished the dressings, I explain to the grandfather through the interpreter that we are trying to gain authority for the child's admission to Camp Bastion. Thanking me, he goes with the interpreter to sleep on the roof of the base.

The doc spends much of that evening on the satellite phone, trying to convince med ops that the child needs a hospital bed, but to no avail. The child does not meet the criteria stipulated in the eligibility matrix that will permit her to be treated in a military medical facility. It is apparent that the best solution is for her to be taken by taxi to the Red Cross hospital in Kandahar.

The following morning, while the doc is back out on the ground with the company, I await confirmation through the civil-military co-operation (CIMIC) team that the Red Cross hospital is willing to take her. It is mid-morning before we have the answer, which is in the affirmative. As with the boy with the eye injury, the plan is for a referral letter and taxi to Kandahar. With the interpreter, I make my way to the roof of the house to speak with the old man.

I explain the situation to him, but before I can explain about the taxi and the hospital, the look on his face betrays a reserved hostility. I can do nothing for him; we have generated false hope, wasted his time and brought him miles from his village to tell him so. He wraps the child in a carrying sling, hoists her in a matter-of-fact way over his shoulder and prepares to leave. I hurriedly explain about the ICRC in Kandahar and give the letter to the grandfather to take. The CIMIC liaison officer who has accompanied me gives the old man fifty dollars. Not a word is said. Shortly afterwards, the disgruntled grandfather leaves via the front gate.

I am disappointed that the doctor did not conduct a proper examination and gain an accurate history in the field, heartbroken that I cannot do more for a desperately sick child and very unhappy that I have been left with the burden of conveying the bad news that is someone else's task to deliver. Worst of all, I feel that I have been let down by a colleague and old friend.

19 FINAL EXCURSION

At the conclusion of the operation in the Upper Sangin Valley, I return with my small band of reinforcements to Camp Bastion. In a matter of days I am flown out to take command of the medical detachment at Now Zad. With the town of Musa Q'aleh still in enemy hands, Now Zad is the most far-flung outpost of the British presence in Helmand and it's a fifty-minute helicopter ride north from Camp Bastion.

The helicopter landing site at Now Zad is situated on a billiard table-flat expanse of desert just outside the town. Approaching the landing site just before dusk, we go through the usual drill of kitting up before the wheels go down so that the helicopter is on the ground for the least possible amount of time. The knowledge that the Taliban have mortared the desert landing site several times adds to the sense of vulnerability that I feel while we're in the open. While we disembark from the helicopter and transfer our kit and ourselves onto ground vehicles, the WMIK Landrovers of the fire support group are deployed in a protective screen around the landing site. As we make the short journey to the base, our tyres throwing up clouds of lunar-like dust, the entire scene is bathed in a reddish hue from the sun as it rapidly slips behind the mountains to the west.

The base is centred on a large house and several outbuildings which lie within a large compound of about two hundred square metres, with sangars built into each corner of the surrounding rectangular wall. I am given a quick orientation. The medical facility is in the main building, next door to the operations room. The briefing room and dining area are in the main hallway. Opposite the ops room and medical facility is a TV room.

Forty men are accommodated in the outbuildings, whilst about thirty more, mainly from the heavy machine gun, mortar sections and fire support team, are based on a rocky outcrop outside the town that provides a vantage point from which most of the town can be seen. This outcrop is known as ANP Hill, (named after the Afghan national police who presumably used to garrison it). The garrison at Now Zad is a 'company minus' group, consisting of 11 Platoon from C Company, elements of the fire support group and other additions. Although I have worked with some of the men during my time at Kajaki, many faces are new.

The two medics in my team are both familiar; each of them worked for me in the Kajaki dream team on separate occasions. I know them both well and am certain of their abilities and limitations. It's necessary to base a medic on ANP Hill in order to support the troops there, and I decide that the best option will be to use both men, rotating them on a three-day turnaround.

Once again we have the luxury of a chef from the Royal Logistic corps, who provides us with two cooked meals each day. Lunch is the usual selection of army biscuits with pâté or some of the warm-weather supplement rations that have become available recently – little luxuries like tuna or noodles in a vacuum-sealed pack. Because the usual chocolate bars have a habit of liquefying in the heat, the vegetable oil separating from the cocoa and milk and leaking through the packet seals, they have been replaced by flapjack bars. If we are really fortunate, we might have sachets of Lucozade Sport to boost our electrolytes and make the chlorinated drinking water taste better.

Once again showering is limited to solar bags, and the sanitary facilities are that old favourite, the oil-drum latrine. The ration-pack food and constant fight for hydration means that bowel movements come only once every three days, but when a man's got to go, a man's got to go! I have been at Now Zad for three days and am engaged in just this activity, when the quiet of the late afternoon is pierced by the shrill wail of the mortar attack alarm. I have two options: leg it from the latrine with a shitty arse, or remain enthroned and finish what I've started with the knowledge that should a mortar bomb land nearby, I might be found dead with my trousers round my ankles and covered in human filth. I choose the latter option. Fortunately, the incoming fire falls wide of the perimeter wall and explodes in a nearby abandoned building.

The biggest challenge at Now Zad is passing the time. Whilst Now Zad was once a hive of activity, patrolling has been reduced in recent months; as a consequence, we have seen a corresponding drop in enemy hostilities, with the exception of the occasional mortar attack. I spend my time reading, writing and taking exercise, using the very basic gym equipment that is housed in one of the outbuildings.

On one of the days that the medics are swapping over, I accompany the resupply run to ANP Hill. The living conditions there are very basic; the men live in sandbag-lined bunkers and dug-outs. I am reminded of images from the western front in the Great War, the difference here being the lack of rain. As I am walking among the weapon pits and bunkers, a piece of high-tech equipment sounds a warning that there is enemy mortar fire inbound. A soldier calls to me, telling me to get into cover. As well as alerting us to the impending danger, the gizmo even provides the coordinates of the enemy firing point.

While we take cover, the mortar teams man their barrels and prepare the counter-fire mission. Within seconds, our mortar barrels are pouring high-explosive ammunition onto the Taliban mortar line. The enemy mortar bombs land off-target; ours do not. Despite the inaccuracy of the enemy fire, one cannot afford the luxury of nonchalance. We are weeks away from the end of tour and nobody wants to be the last man wounded or killed.

The number of casualties I'm required to treat is mercifully low. I evacuate one soldier as a non-emergency case; this young man was hit by splinters from an enemy mortar bomb. The fragments of metal casing are embedded too deep for me to remove and he requires surgery. As there is no helicopter lift scheduled for several days, I discuss his case with a doctor via a satellite phone. We agree that it is appropriate for me to treat him conservatively with wound dressings supported by prophylactic intravenous antibiotics.

A more serious casualty whom I treat is an elderly Afghan man who has been shot through the chest with a pistol. We are told by his grandson that he has been shot by the Taliban because they believe he is spying for the coalition. None of us knows if this is true or if we are being told this story because it is what the grandson thinks we want to hear. However, if the background story is uncertain, his need for medical treatment is not. We treat him by applying a dressing to the exit wound and a chest seal to the entry wound. Although the man is stable, I opt to get IV access in controlled circumstances now, rather than struggling in an emergency at a later time. Because the man's injury was caused by hostile action, we are able to obtain a bed for him at the Camp Bastion field hospital and evacuate him within the hour.

Several days later, I fall ill with a severe flu-like viral illness that sees me feverish and delirious. For thirty-six hours I lie flat-out on my camp cot, taking paracetamol tablets and drinking as much water as I can without feeling nauseous. One of the DVD box sets that I've watched recently was

'Sharpe's Rifles', the 1990s TV dramatisation of Bernard Cornwell's novels, starring Sean Bean. In my delirious state I am lost in time and place, my dreams merging the fiction of Napoleonic-era combat with current events in Afghanistan. It is surreal, to say the least.

While I'm still recovering from the viral illness I am stung by a large wasp, immediately feeling the tell-tale swelling on my leg where I have been stung. I take an immediate dose of antihistamine and anti-inflammatory medication. It does the trick; ever since my experience with scorpion-man at Kajaki, I am paranoid about anaphylaxis.

Although our area is largely quiet there remains some activity, including a sniper who makes a nuisance of himself. Following the principle of setting a thief to catch a thief, the sniper platoon is flown in to eliminate the errant sharpshooter. It is exciting stuff, but comes to nothing as the quarry fails to show himself for the duration of the anti-sniper operation.

It is mid-October and we are at the end of our tour. Troops from 40 Commando, Royal Marines begin arriving to conduct a relief-in-place. The British commander is replaced by a captain from the United States Marine corps, who is on an exchange posting with the Royal Marines. He is an interesting and likeable guy; he has already acquired a touch of the classic British sense of irony and has some interesting tales to tell from his time in Fallujah. Before long it is my turn to leave. I will be replaced by Joanne, a fellow nursing officer whom I have known for thirteen years. I leave a reasonably comprehensive set of handover notes and sign off with wishes of good luck for her tour.

In a reversal of my arrival at Now Zad, we are driven out to the desert landing site. Two Chinooks land, throwing up dust clouds and pelting us with stones. As I approach the tail ramp of my lift home, I look across and see Joanne in new desert combat uniform, stepping off from the tail ramp of the other helicopter. She's too far away for me to see her face, but her body language speaks volumes; the tail ramp of her helicopter represents the last connection with home and it looks as though she's getting to grips with adjusting to her new environment.

On board the Chinook, I ditch my Bergen rucksack and sit down on the canvas seating, strapping myself in. The airframe judders and rocks forward as the helicopter lifts off. I pray for an uneventful flight; it would be really bad luck to crash or be shot down now.

Fortunately, my final Chinook ride in Afghanistan passes without event and I land at Camp Bastion in the early afternoon, where I'm picked up by a Land Rover. Returning to Brydon Lines, I clamber off the tail-gate and heave my kit into the headquarters tent. The handover-takeover with our successors from 5 General Support medical regiment is already well under way, to the extent that I barely recognise anyone in the command post. I find out where I am going to be living for my last few days in country, but moving my kit there will have to wait.

The word goes around that Commander 12 Mechanised Brigade, Brigadier John Lorimer has arrived at the medical group headquarters and wishes to address us before he leaves for the UK later today. The brigadier is ebullient and effusive in the words of gratitude that he conveys. He thanks us all for our hard work and tells us he realises that some of us are only just in from the field; the good brigadier chooses this moment to single me out and places me in this category by complimenting me on my beard. He implores us always to remember the good work that we have done here and the lives that we have saved. It feels good to be valued.

After the brigadier and his entourage leave, I return to the job at hand of prepping myself to return home. I start with a deep clean of my rifle. Despite my having been meticulous about daily cleaning, six months of exposure to Afghan dust has taken its toll and there is significant sand ingress into the deeper recesses of the weapon. I can now do more than a basic field-strip and really dig into the nooks and crannies. After an hour, my rifle is practically sparkling. The last thing I do is to apply a generous coating of oil onto all the bearing surfaces and pull the barrel through with a lightly oiled square of cotton flannelette. It will be days, if not weeks, before I see my rifle again and it will 'sweat' in transit, so the oil is required to protect the metal from rusting.

That evening, I meet some friends from C Company at the outside dining area adjacent to our camp. The Pizza Hut trailer is finally open and doing a roaring trade. It is amazing to think that here in Camp Bastion and also at Kandahar, some soldiers' Afghanistan experience really does consist of frequent visits to Pizza Hut, Costa Coffee and Tim Horton's, just to break up the boredom of being in a large open prison in a foreign land. It is great to see the lads from C Company and have the chance to shoot the breeze with them in an environment with no immediate threat to our lives.

The next day marks a key milestone in the journey home. After breakfast, I report to hand in my operational equipment: my rifle, 350 rounds of ammunition, two morphine auto-injectors, combat tourniquets, patrol medical pack and body armour. To hand over the body armour, I have to remove the Kevlar plates and the flexible poly-aramid filler from the cover so that each item can be accounted for. As I dismantle my body armour, I am shocked to find that six months of sweat, combined with the acidic dirt to which the cover has been exposed, has rotted and weakened much of the stitching. The fabric cover literally falls apart at the seams.

The squadron quartermaster sergeant and his team take back all my equipment and rip up my Army Form 1033 loan voucher. As I step away from the trestle table, the most amazing sense of relief washes over me. I have made it; I have survived my six months in Afghanistan with body, mind and spirit largely intact. It is not until I'm relieved of the burden of responsibility for myself, my medics and our patients that I realise how heavily it has weighed upon me.

For the time being, I will not have to jump from deep sleep to treating a seriously ill or wounded patient. I won't be required to run through a wall of enemy fire to reach a wounded man. I am unlikely to be maimed or killed just by being in the wrong place at the wrong time. I won't have to allocate troops to task, deciding which of my team goes to the platoon entrusted with the most dangerous task of a mission and which will remain in the relative safety of the company sergeant-major's party or stay at the base. I think of the sights and sounds of the previous six months: the good men killed, the young lads who have lost limbs or been wounded in other ways. Tears begin to well up but I don't allow them to fall, not here, not now. Save it for later, I tell myself.

Over the next couple of days, the various medical teams filter in from the outstations as they are replaced and go through the same process of de-kitting and admin. Eventually, along with about a hundred colleagues, it is my turn to fly by C-130 transport to Kandahar and begin the long journey home. There are delays and the inevitable 'fuck around' factor whereby confusion reigns about when we will actually leave Afghanistan. Dave, a good friend who is acting as our squadron commander, arranges for me to get away on an earlier flight than the one for which I am earmarked. I feel bad for leaving early, but Dave tells me that he has no need of me and I've earned my early passage home.

Many hours later, on a damp and drizzly October morning, I land at RAF Brize Norton in Oxfordshire with a free can of beer, courtesy of the Royal Air Force. As I push my trolley through the arrivals gate, I am met by a driver from my unit who will take me and the other medical personnel on my flight back to our barracks in Aldershot. My tour has come to an end.

20 ADJUSTMENT

The army has a policy for soldiers returning from operations, known as normalisation. The first stage of this is decompression, which involves a stopover at one of the British Sovereign base areas in Cyprus.

Decompression is a combination of military administration, organised fun and a reintroduction to alcohol consumption in a controlled environment. The whole idea is aimed at reducing post-operational stress and discipline problems by providing a pressure release before soldiers go home, the idea being to prevent them from getting into drunken fights as soon as they return. Whilst decompression may be of some benefit, I'm not convinced that it is entirely effective. More than a century may have passed since Rudyard Kipling penned 'Tommy', his timeless tribute to the British soldier, but single men in barracks remain unlikely plaster saints and their 'conduck' is definitely not always 'fancy paints'. To use a barrelful of clichés: drink is drink, boys will be boys, the nice (and not so nice) girls will always love a soldier and their boyfriends will usually get jealous. Whether or not you let the boys have a few beers in Cyprus, there will still be hassles when they finally get back to the UK.

When we return to Browning barracks, a small welcoming committee of regimental personnel and families are there to meet us. Before I go anywhere or do anything, I have to hand in my weapon ancillaries: cleaning kit, rifle magazines, bayonet and scabbard. There is a little bit of administration to be done and then I am free to go - not on leave, but for a long weekend. Lisa drives me home where we have a small celebration of my homecoming.

As the remainder of the regiment comes home over the next two weeks, we are kept occupied with low-key work aimed at reintroducing us to normal life. There are sports competitions, social functions, a regimental photograph and a service at the garrison church. Although it is now late October and the weather is damp and cold, we continue to wear our desert combat uniforms in accordance with policy for units returning from operations. I think that this is so that we can be recognised as returning heroes. Once we have been normalised, we are free to go on leave: five weeks initially, followed by a week back at work for the army's rituals of pre-Christmas celebrations. There is an 'officers' mess vs warrant officers and sergeants' mess' football match, 'officers' mess to warrant officers and sergeants' mess' exchange of drinks and a junior ranks' Christmas luncheon, which sees them waited upon by the officers and sergeants. This last event usually sees more than a few Brussels sprouts being used as indirect fire. All in all, it's good fun. After the silly season we go on leave for Christmas itself, returning to work in mid-January.

During my time off I become a house-husband, caring for my baby boy and two stepdaughters while my wife goes to work. Intending to write about my experiences, I find that between washing, cooking, cleaning, nappy changes and the school runs, my days disappear, leaving me no time to do so. I am also beginning to discover the toll that six months on operations has taken on my body, mind and spirit. I'm exhausted and find myself sleepwalking through each day, longing for the moment when I can return to bed. It is as though each of the energy slumps that I experienced following an adrenalin surge on the battlefield was a mere precursor to the fatigue I now experience. If I let myself, I could drift on a sea of exhaustion to the ends of the world and beyond. I'm utterly drained.

A few days after my return, I open my large holdall and Bergen rucksack with the intention of sorting out my kit.

Opening the bags, I am hit by the unforgettable smell of Afghanistan. The musky odour of desert sand and stale sweat overpowers my senses and I am immediately transported from leafy suburbia to a dun-coloured, bomb-blasted compound in Helmand, where I am fighting to save the life of an ashen-faced youth, the air around me thick with acrid smoke and the rattle of small-arms fire carried on the breeze. The vividness of the scene that unfolded in my head having taken me by surprise, I close the bags and take a few moments to compose myself. Picking up Pandora's holdall and rucksack, I throw them back into the box room to leave them for another day.

Over the following months, I am constantly ill. By the time of my return to work in January, I succumb to flu-like symptoms every Friday afternoon, recovering in time for work on Monday. This goes on until March, when the symptoms are so severe that I am admitted to hospital. I spend a week at Frimley Park hospital, being submitted to all the investigations that the consultant physician can think of. When all the tests come back negative, I know what I don't have but the cause of my recurrent illness remains a mystery. I am discharged, and after a month of rest begin to feel like my old self. I am running every day and have the strength to do some gardening. I am physically on the road to recovery but, as I later discover, there are some monsters hiding in my subconscious which have yet to make their presence known.

Eighteen months post-tour, I'm plagued by nightmares and flashbacks and have developed a quick temper. I book in to see the doctor and request a referral to the mental health services. For a period of about three months, I see a civilian mental health nurse named Matt. Matt reassures me that I am not mad and have simply experienced some extreme life events. I concur. We have a few counselling sessions, and it seems that the events during the raid on

Mazdurak are central to my problems. Matt asks me to write an operational-style report of the raid, the idea being to encourage' me to think about the events in a dispassionate way. This leads him to take me through a program of eye-movement desensitisation therapy. Don't ask me to explain how this works, but it does seem to be effective. During the course of the therapy it becomes apparent that the most likely cause of my symptoms was the act of burying terrifying thoughts and emotions deep into my subconscious to enable me to do my job. Although I feel much better and manage to get discharged from the psych. clinic, I'm still not fully recovered.

Four years later, I have been promoted to major and have responsibility for the management of a team of thirty military nurses working on the surgical wards of a large NHS Hospital in Portsmouth. The ward is over-stretched and under-resourced, which results in a high-stress environment; it is not uncommon for distressed male patients to cry out in pain, which transports me back to Helmand. There are days when the mental and emotional demands made upon nurses in this environment are almost on par with those of the battlefield. In my mind, Mazdurak has become the yardstick by which I measure how tough a day I'm having.

One weekend I purchase a copy of the *Sunday Telegraph*. In one of the supplements, there's a piece about modern war poetry written by British soldiers who served in Iraq and Afghanistan. As I read the article, it emerges that there is a competition to select poems for an anthology of modern war poetry. The panel of judges will be General the Lord Dannatt (former chief of the general staff), Carol-Ann Duffy (poet laureate), Simon Duffy (former presenter of *Poetry Please* on BBC Radio 4) and John Jeffcock (poet, entrepreneur and former captain in the Coldstream Guards). The project is John's brainchild. I am hooked.

I write a number of poems over the course of that weekend, the first of which tells the story of the raid on Mazdurak. It joins the action at the point after C and A have been evacuated and focusses on the hectic events in the walled garden compound. I make a couple of amendments and give it a title: 'Care Under Fire'. Writing the poem proves cathartic and I feel that it has helped exorcise some of the demons that stayed behind to fight a rear-guard action following my time with the psych. team. I submit all my Afghanistan poems to the competition.

A poem entitled 'In Memoriam' is my tribute to the memory of Dave Hicks, who was awarded a posthumous Military Cross for his gallantry in attempting to continue to lead the men of C Company in the defence of patrol base Inkerman, despite being mortally wounded. 'Courageous Restraint on R&R' seeks to put the reader into the position of a young soldier who resists the temptation to get into a bar brawl during his two weeks at home from Helmand. The poem is not written with anyone in mind, but had my nineteen-year-old self been deployed to Afghanistan, it might have been about me.

After a wait of several months, I am pleased to discover that all my poems have made the cut. Invited to attend the book launch at the Cavalry and Guards club in Piccadilly in November 2011, I have the pleasure of meeting John Jeffcock and a number of the other poets. John introduces me to a young guy named Matt, who works for BBC TV and is very keen to interview me about my poetry for the *One Show*, a weekday magazine show that airs at 6 p.m.

After jumping through hoops with my chain of command, Matt and his team interview me on camera and film me reading an extract from 'Care Under Fire'. The interview airs the following day. Unfortunately *Top Gear* presenter Jeremy Clarkson is also interviewed for a different topic on the same show and famously comments that public service workers who are on strike should be 'shot in front of their families'. Whilst this has no impact on the success of the book launch, it does mean that this particular episode of the *One Show* never makes it onto BBC iPlayer.

Twelve months after the publication of the anthology, I receive an email from BBC Radio 4's *The Today Show*, inviting me to be interviewed about modern war poetry. The email arrives on a Thursday evening and the producer wants me to come to the studio in London on Saturday morning. There isn't enough time between the arrival of the email and the filming of the show to obtain the necessary permission from the army to be interviewed. To say that I'm disappointed is an understatement. Radio 4 is the station of choice for thinking Britain, and *Today* is its flagship morning current affairs show; I have been an avid listener for years. Life is too short to deal in 'what ifs', but I do occasionally wonder what might have happened had I been able to accept the invitation for an interview.

My time in Afghanistan has left an indelible mark upon my soul. Although there were some very near misses, I came home in one piece, which I sometimes find miraculous. To the outside world, I came home without a scratch; nevertheless, I was wounded inside. My mental wounds have largely healed, but scars will always remain. That's the thing about scar tissue: it grows fibrous, thick and gristly to heal the wound, but never acts in quite the same way as the original tissue it replaces.

POST SCRIPT

In 2014, my teenage stepdaughter decided to install Wattpad on my iPhone, informing me that it might be good for my writing. I had no idea what Wattpad was for. It wasn't until I had a good look at the app that I decided to upload my poetry; not just the Afghanistan collection, but also some older poems from my younger days in the Army. I have also written some non-war poetry and now this story, which I had tried and failed to write so many times before. Most importantly, I know that I now produce work that is being read and appreciated, even if only by a small audience. I draw comfort from knowing that nothing I write will now sit in a drawer gathering dust for more than a decade. For that I have to thank all of my wonderful readers who encourage me in my writing.

Despite my worst fears, all of the men wounded in the raid on Mazdurak survived.

C was flown back to the UK for treatment, I last saw him at the Battalion's Minden Day celebration in 2007, to which I was kindly invited while I was on R&R from Afghanistan.

A had severe head injuries and lost his right eye. Last time I saw him was at the Grenadier Guards memorial service held in the Royal Garrison Church, Aldershot in the autumn of 2007. He was wearing an eye-patch which somehow seemed to suit him. A greeted me with the words, "All right, sir, how're you doing? I was in shit-state last time you saw me, wasn't I?" A had received a significant pay-out in compensation and insurance for the loss of his eye, which he invested in a very flash car that he apparently kept crashing due to the resulting lack of depth perception. It was a genuine pleasure to see him.

S had severe fragmentation injuries to his heart and lungs. The danger of a tension pneumothorax – a life-threatening complication of chest trauma – that had worried me in the walled garden compound came to pass, but only after he had gone through surgery. I last saw S in 2008, when I invited him and some of the other Mazdurak casualties to talk about their experiences to new medics undergoing their trade training. S still has fragments in his heart and lungs, because the surgeons in the Camp Bastion field hospital and at the Queen Elizabeth hospital in Birmingham felt that to attempt to remove them represented a grave risk to his life. I have seen him featured in several national newspaper reports, one of which described his insurance pay-out as a pittance because it was not loss of a limb or an eye. If this is true, it is shameful treatment of a young man who has given so much in the service of his country.

N underwent surgery in Camp Bastion and the UK. He returned to operations in Afghanistan later that summer. When I got the chance to speak to him, I reminded him of his refusal to accept pain relief and commented that it must have required big balls. His response, "Oh, no, it wasn't that I didn't need it, sir. I'm just terrified of needles!"

Either way, it was still a gutsy call. I haven't seen N since, but a couple of years ago I saw his name published on the army promotions board results as having been promoted to sergeant.

For some time after that tour, I kept the kneepads and desert boots that I had been wearing that day, all of them covered with the rusty-brown blood that N had shed. After I had the counselling and therapy, I didn't know why I was still holding onto them. They went in the bin.

Medic Matt didn't return to operations that summer, his injuries being more complex than anyone realised at the time. A Royal Anglian regimental combat medical technician, he has since been transferred into the Royal Army Medical Corps. Last time I saw him, he had been promoted to sergeant and was in charge of the Vikings' regimental aid post.

Steve is still in the army and doing very well. I had the pleasure and privilege to attend his wedding the year after the Afghan summer of love. I have not seen Steve since, but he wrote a stunning account of my actions in Mazdurak which was read out to the members of the Queen Alexandra's Royal Army Nursing Corps headquarters officers' mess on the occasion of my being 'dined out' at the end of my service. Hearing Steve's account read aloud made me blush.

Beyond the violence and chaos that I witnessed in Afghanistan, some of my most vivid memories are the small acts of kindness and the great acts of selflessness that I witnessed so many times. Tommo dishing out cigarettes to his men in the aftermath of the Raid on Mazdurak is a prime example of the former; of the latter, there are so many examples that I could not choose one over the others. Both great and small acts are the outer manifestation of what I have come to view as a form of love. This is the kind of love that causes men to throw themselves onto grenades to save their comrades, that makes them carry a wounded man across open ground under withering fire or prompts a wounded man to walk back to the aid post to save his comrades the hard work of carrying him. I saw that love manifest itself so many times in the summer of 2007, but few people embodied it more than Steve. Months after the raid on Mazdurak, Steve showed me something he had kept to himself. It was the backpack and combat trousers he had been wearing the morning he had carried A back to safety. The backpack had two or three bullet-holes in it; alarmingly, the lower legs of the combat trousers also had a couple of bullet-holes: the final miracle of the raid on Mazdurak. Steve, wherever you are, stay safe; you will always be like a brother to me.

POETRY

Three poems from the 'Heroes' anthology

CARE UNDER FIRE

Fast jets scream in with cannon and bomb, breaking up the enemy attack
Blast reverberates through my entire being, rendering me deaf and dazed
Beneath my body armour a film of mud and dust lies gritty against my skin
An explosion rips through the compound, followed by shouts of 'man down'

I have been a spectator in this gallery of hellish images, now my work begins
I believe the first man is dead, rolling him to check brings a low animalistic groan
With help from two of his mates, we drag him into cover
I start to check him over when I am told of another casualty

'That's four this morning.' 'How many more?'
'Are we going to get out of this alive?' 'Will I be next?'
Unanswered questions left hanging, pushed to the back of the mind
Get on with the job at hand

The village is shrouded in smoke and fire as the company fights for its life
Surrounded by comrades in this maelstrom of battle, I am alone
Sheltering in the lee of a compound wall as if from a mighty storm, ignoring the chaos
I kneel between the two living corpses and start my battle for their lives

Ashen faced and pallid, if I don't act fast he will bleed out
Reaching into my map pocket I pull out an emergency care bandage

Sweating, shaky hands fumble and slip on the glossy plastic wrapper
Gripping it with my teeth I rip it open and the grey and white roll is free

Pressing the white pad against the groin and wrapping it tight, I stem the flow of blood
Binding his legs with cas straps and a jimpy sling*, all seems good, radial pulse present
'No morphine, boss', he tells me. I turn to the other man, he is getting worse
Gasping for breath with a look of terror in his eyes

Removing his body armour shows the peppering where a thousand minute metal shards have ripped through flesh and sinew, crushing lung, lacerating vessels
The chest seal will not stick, it slides on a body slick with sweat and blood, I inwardly curse the maker of a device not fit for purpose. Go for a chest drain or leave it?

Sitting him upright brings an improvement - leave it for later - dress his other wounds
Unwell, but not getting worse, I am winning my battle - I pause and observe the other

An overheated barrel brings a machine gun to a stop; 'Who needs a piss?' the gunner asks
Three men stand over the barrel, streams sizzle on the hot metal and vaporise
The stench of urine mingles with hot oil and gun smoke; a sharp tang in the back of the throat
The gun roars back into life to cover our extraction, carrying stretchers out under fire

Two live casualties are strapped to the CSM's quad bike and taken to meet the helicopter
I have earned my pay and return to my role as spectator,

the amateur playing soldier
Once contact is broken I trudge back to camp at the rear
of the platoon
A film of the action replays in my head, I hope I have
done enough

In camp, a debrief, rifle cleaned, med kit replenished and
scoff
Minimise in force - can't phone home; even if I could,
what would I say?
Sleep comes hard, tears are shed, images of the wounded
on my mind
A prayer for the boys on patrol tomorrow and the ones
that are left behind

*Jimpy sling: General Purpose Machine Gun (GPMG)
sling

IN MEMORIAM

News of your death came in fragments
The news told me a 'Viking' had fallen
I heard on the grapevine it was C Company
At KAF I found out it was you

I shall never forget you, who made a stranger welcome
Unflappable in the ops room, managing chaos
Shirt off, cigarette lit, sporting a boyish grin
Combat took you before smoking could

I should have been there
Could have tried to save you
Would it have made a difference?
Would being there have changed anything?

I saw your repatriation
Met your parents
Laid Minden Roses at your grave
Is it not enough?

Does time really heal?
Four years have passed
Memory of you has not
Eternally young and courageous

You earned your peace
Have I?

COURAGEOUS RESTRAINT ON R&R

Long days in the pub
Mates at work
Drinking too much again
Time on my hands
Killing hands killing time

Beery bonhomie starts to grate
Turns into something else
A sneery comment, a nasty jibe
Fists fly furiously
Punches thrown first, followed by glasses

Rage descends
Head makes contact with nose
Right uppercut, a sickening crunch
Elbow to face, knee to groin
The fat civilian slides to the floor
Just desserts

Composure recovered; fix him with a steely glare
The fight a fleeting fantasy, what might have been
I think I had better leave
In the dark street the leaves whirl and scratch at the lamp-posts
At home, in Helmand, courageous restraint is never easy

ABOUT THE AUTHOR

After qualifying as a registered nurse in the NHS, Barry Alexander joined the army and served for twenty years in the Queen Alexandra's Royal Army Nursing Corps, retiring as Major in 2014. His poetry has been published in the 2011 anthology 'Heroes: 100 Poems from the New Generation of War Poets' (Ebury Press).

Printed in Great Britain
by Amazon